Series 07-052

USING MICROCOMPUTERS IN RESEARCH

THOMAS WM. MADRON
C. NEAL TATE
ROBERT G. BROOKSHIRE
North Texas State University

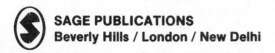

SAGE PUBLICATIONS
Beverly Hills / London / New Delhi

For information address:

SAGE Publications, Inc.
275 South Beverly Drive
Beverly Hills, California 90212

SAGE Publications India Pvt. Ltd.
M-32 Market Greater Kailash I
New Delhi 110 048, India

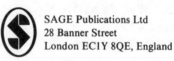

SAGE Publications Ltd
28 Banner Street
London EC1Y 8QE, England

International Standard Book Number 0-8039-2457-7

Library of Congress Catalog Card No. 85-050305

SECOND PRINTING, 1986

When citing a professional paper, please use the proper form. Remember to cite the
correct Sage University Paper series title and include the paper number. One of the
following formats can be adapted (depending on the style manual used):

(1) IVERSEN, GUDMUND R. and NORPOTH, HELMUT (1976) "Analysis of
Variance." Sage University Paper series on Quantitative Applications in the Social
Sciences, 07-001. Beverly Hills and London: Sage Pubns.

OR

(2) Iversen, Gudmund R. and Norpoth, Helmut. 1976. *Analysis of Variance.* Sage
University Paper series on Quantitative Applications in the Social Sciences, series no.
07-001. Beverly Hills and London: Sage Pubns.

CONTENTS

Series Editor's Introduction

In this book, the authors consider the many ways in which microcomputers can be used to expedite both quantitative and non-quantitative research. This volume should be read with the earlier book in this series, *Microcomputer Methods for Social Scientists,* by Philip Schrodt. Together they provide a lucid and comprehensive introduction to microcomputing in the social sciences.

This monograph is organized around the research process. Chapter 1 presents microcomputer hardware, software, and terminology. Chapter 2 begins with a discussion of the use of microcomputers in the first stage of most research projects, the research proposal. Here microcomputers are used as word processors to decrease the time spent in organizing and producing a proposal. They greatly facilitate the insertion of "boiler plate" text common to many of these documents, they speed the communication of drafts among co-authors, and they simplify the process of revision. The features of word processing programs are discussed here, and six of these packages are compared.

If a research proposal is accepted, the researcher is faced with the problem of creating and managing a budget. In Chapter 3 the authors introduce the spreadsheet program, a tool developed for business budgeting and forecasting. The characteristics of these programs are described, and detailed examples are presented to demonstrate their usefulness.

Microcomputers can also be used as data collection tools. In Chapter 4, the authors demonstrate the use of file and data base management programs for copying and organizing notes. Naturally, word processing makes the construction of questionnaires and survey instruments easier, and data collection can be controlled and monitored by microcomputers with the use of computer aided telephone interviewing software. In field research, portable and transportable microcomputers can bring computer technology to the site of research. In small group research, microcomputers can provide both process control and measurement tools.

In data collection, information must often be communicated quickly and accurately between researchers and to other facilities for analysis. Chapter 4 describes communications hardware and software that can facilitate this process, and also introduces more specialized uses of local area networks, voice-based computer communications and mainframe disk storage.

In Chapter 5, the role of microcomputers in data analysis is discussed. The authors present the advantages and disadvantages of conducting statistical analysis on microcomputers, and move on to a discussion of the use of word processing programs in writing the research report. They discuss programs that can check spelling and typographical errors, correct grammatical mistakes, act as an "electronic" thesaurus, and generate indexes and tables of contents. These are all important aids for the researcher.

This volume can provide the reader with a heightened appreciation of the usefulness of microcomputers in research, an application that will become more important as microcomputers become ubiquitous in our universities, colleges, governmental agencies, businesses, and homes. It will be extremely helpful for introducing both undergraduate and graduate students to the use of microcomputers throughout the research process.

—John L. Sullivan
Series Co-Editor

USING MICROCOMPUTERS IN RESEARCH

THOMAS WM. MADRON
C. NEAL TATE
ROBERT G. BROOKSHIRE
North Texas State University

1. MICROCOMPUTERS AND THE RESEARCH PROCESS

Microcomputers are the fundamental building blocks of the information revolution. As scientists and researchers, we are contributing to that revolution. It is imperative that we improve the level of our productivity or we will be overwhelmed by the information we need to process. This book is about the use of microcomputers in the research process.

Just as Gutenberg's rediscovery of movable type in the mid-fifteenth century brought about widespread literacy (and, therefore, improved personal productivity) by making printed materials widely and cheaply available, so in the 1980s microcomputers are bringing about the ability to deal better with the large quantities of information that we all must confront. Because there is so much information, however, the researcher is having ever greater demands placed on his or her time. Demands to produce results more quickly are becoming insistent.

The growth in the use of microcomputers in research will change the way in which research has been accomplished since at least the 1940s. Because of the cost of large mainframe computers, scientists and scholars were required to work within the framework of large organizations: universities, corporations, and governments. With the expanding capabilities of micros, and their declining costs, it is once more possible (or soon will be) to do significant research without the need for extensive infrastructures. It may again come about that the ideal of the classical scholar working alone in his or her study may be realized

7

through the uses of the new technology. This is not to say that all researchers will want to work in scholarly isolation, and for those who do not, microcomputers can facilitate research as well. It does mean, however, that individuals can have the kinds of resources that have only been available to large organizations up to now.

Microcomputers are so popular because they have an extraordinarily broad range of applications. They are, of course, widely used in business for data processing, accounting, and other traditional computer tasks, but personal computers are also becoming standard tools in such diverse areas as elementary education, farming and ranching, architectural design, legal and medical practice, and real estate. The object of this book is to show that micros have a place in all stages and types of research, as well.

The organization of this volume reflects this focus. After a brief introduction that will explain the basic structure of the microcomputer, and define some microcomputer jargon, we will approach each step in the research process, from the initial search of the literature to the submission of the final report for publication. We will suggest ways in which a microcomputer can make each of these steps better, easier, and faster. Use of micros by researchers has the potential to expand productivity, which will enable scholars to take on larger and more complex projects as well as increasing the quality and quantity of output, at the same time enabling them to cope with the increasing demands of the information revolution.

Why Use a Computer At All?

Microcomputers can be the cornerstone in improved research productivity because of the tasks that they allow us to perform faster, better, and more efficiently. They are among the first of many personal productivity tools that will rapidly become available to us all during the mid to late 80s. How is all this possible? It is possible because microcomputers are uniquely personal tools. They are devices that encourage us to make better use of our time, and have the potential for making the time we spend at work more interesting and pleasant.

Although microcomputers come in small packages, they are by no means trivial machines. They have the speed of many mainframe computers of the 1960s and 1970s. The capabilities of the large machines of that era are frequently dwarfed by microcomputers hardly larger than an electronic typewriter. Some modern microcomputers have memory capacities that exceed those of earlier machines. They have software options that exceed the choices available to users of large mainframes of the 60s and 70s, or for that matter, even of the 80s.

By the mid-1980s microcomputers were very much in evidence in universities and research laboratories. It was clear that in order to do their job properly, researchers needed to process information better. At the same time some people found, in their attempts to use centralized, large-scale computing services, that the level of service offered by a central facility frequently left something to be desired. When people are asked why they want to use microcomputers in the workplace, a frequently heard response is that they want independence from central computing facilities.

Independence from central computing facilities often is seen not solely in terms of displeasure with the cost, quality, or variety of services provided. Some of the services being demanded are often not even available on central site computers, and microcomputer software is typically easier to use than corresponding software on the large central mainframe, even if corresponding services are available.

Another reason for the adoption of microcomputers was economy. It may sound strange to suggest that a microcomputer costing four, five or six thousand dollars is more economical than a simple terminal. But many of the terminals used in large organizations are not inexpensive. An inexpensive micro configuration is often less expensive than a "smart" terminal. Being on line to a large mainframe computer system one hundred percent of the time is not particularly cost-effective either. A permanently on-line terminal constantly monopolizes a certain minimum number of resources even when that terminal is not in use— and most terminals are *not* in constant use. A microcomputer can be used as the means for communicating with the mainframe system, when that is desirable.

As we discuss below, microcomputers can be used as intelligent work stations in a distributed processing environment in universities, corporations, and other large research organizations. Researchers often need large data files; they require not only great information storage capacity, but they must have speed in the rate at which the appropriate information is processed. Microcomputers have the ability to act like terminals when connected to a central mainframe system. The intelligence of microcomputers allows micro users to extract subsets of large databases and download those data to a micro for specialized analysis or reporting.

There are also some applications that, although important to the end user, do little more than clutter up large central systems. An excellent example of such an application is word processing. Word processing on large central systems is rarely very efficient, and word processing on smaller minicomputers has the same disadvantage that all systems with central points of failure have: When the central system goes down, everybody is out of work, at least temporarily. Microcomputers in office settings provide an enormous amount of redundancy when used for applications such as word processing. When a microcomputer goes down, it will affect only a single user and there is probably a neighboring micro that can be borrowed. When a larger, more centralized system goes down, it may interfere with the work of a hundred or more people.

When we put all of this together, we can use the microcomputer sitting before us on the desk as a word processor, as a spread sheet for various kinds of analyses, as the manager of small to middle size (with capacities expanding rapidly) data bases transferred from the central system to our local system, and as a point on a larger network servicing our many needs. For a host of applications the use of large computers is something akin to swatting flies with a sledgehammer. It works, but there's a better way. For maximum productivity, we should use computer systems that fit the required processing needs.

What About My Mainframe (or Mini)?

Computers have been traditionally classed as "micros," "minis," or "mainframes," corresponding to small, medium, and large machines. In earlier days of computing the distinctions were also based on the speed, word size, or power of the computers' central processing unit. By the 1980s, these distinctions had all but disappeared; the most powerful micros competed with minis and the most powerful minis competed with mainframes. A more useful distinction is between personal (micro)computers dedicated to one person's use, and centrally administered, multi-user systems (minis and mainframes). Even this distinction is not always useful. Micros can also be configured as multi-user systems.

If we have microcomputers, why do we need the big machines? Contemporary mainframes exceed the speed of micros. Generally the external storage capabilities of mainframe computer systems greatly exceed those of micros. Some data must be centrally managed and maintained and cannot be fully distributed to a large number of small machines. Part of the solution to the need for centralized data lies in networking large numbers of microcomputers, perhaps in tandem with larger mainframe systems, to make better use of the information our organizations collect and maintain. The mainframe will not rapidly disappear in large organizations, although the way in which it is used will change considerably over the next few years. One of the ways in which the large machines will be used is as a peripheral device for microcomputer work stations. Such a use may be of particular value to researchers.

Just as the speed and computing capacity of microcomputers are increasing, so too are the capabilities of mainframes. Processing speed on mainframe computers is often measured in terms of MIPS (millions of instructions per second). In the mid-1980s, mainframes operating in the five to ten MIPS range are common, and "supercomputers" capable of executing hundreds of MIPS are available. We anticipate that computers executing over a thousand MIPS will be available by the end of the decade. Thus, mainframe computers will remain the primary medium for processing large tasks using millions of data records or many complex mathematical operations. The cost of these machines, like their performance, is extraordinary, and will require the resources of large institutions for purchase and maintenance. The capabilities of these machines will extend the range of problems that researchers can address, but will continue to be available only within the context of universities, governments, and corporations.

Some Microcomputer Terminology

To make what has already been said more easily understandable, we'll define a microcomputer and its components. A micro is composed of its central processing unit (CPU), information storage (memory and disks), and devices for communicating with the micro. Communications to or from the micro are conducted via keyboard, a mouse system, displays, printers, and related devices. Micros are often configured so that there are several ways for the human user to send messages to the computer and for the computer to send messages back to its human user. The Apple Macintosh, for example, is sold with both a keyboard and a mouse system for input to the computer, and both a printer and a display screen for output.

ELEMENTS OF A MICROCOMPUTER

The central processing unit (CPU) is the core of the microcomputer. Fundamentally, the CPU is the brain of a computer. It contains the electronic circuits that carry out the instructions given to the computer.

Now, we're going to get just a bit more technical than we've been up to this point. Two terms that you often hear used in conjunction with microcomputers, or for that matter any other computers, are bits and bytes. A *bit* is simply an on or off state recognized by the CPU as being meaningful. A series of such on and off states can represent a set of numbers in binary notation. A *byte* is a collection of bits that contains an instruction or piece of data. The most common byte size, used by many different CPUs, is eight bits long. The eight-bit standard came into early use in computing, and the consequence is that a number of related standards were established using byte lengths of eight bits.

The eight bits of a byte can be arranged in such a fashion so as to provide 256 different and distinct patterns representing the decimal numbers from 0 through 255. The American Standard Code for Information Interchange (ASCII) code defines 128 of these codes (using seven bits), the first 31 of which represent so-called control codes (nonprinting characters). Many applications programs use these codes to direct program operation. The other 97 codes represent all the letters of the standard Latin alphabet in both upper and lower case, the ten Arabic numerals, and a variety of special characters such as commas, periods, and so forth. Figure 1.1 shows the first 128 decimal codes, their ASCII assignments, and the binary codes they represent. The various manufacturers of microcomputers use the remaining 128 characters for a variety of different things, most commonly for defining graphics characters.

In communications applications seven of the bits (those defining the 128 standard characters) are used to encode information, and the last bit is used as a *parity* indicator. The parity bit is used to verify the information contained in the other seven bits. There are several ways in which parity can be used to check the accuracy of transmitted data, the two most common being *odd* and *even*.

In checking parity, the CPU adds up the first seven bits of the byte, and calculates whether the total is odd or even. If odd parity checking is being used, it then adds the appropriate bit, 0 or 1, to make the total for the byte an odd number. In even parity checking, the total for the byte will be an even number. The computer that is receiving the data then carries out its own parity calculations, and compares its parity bit with the bit from the sending machine. If the two do not match, the receiving computer reports a parity error.

The 8-bit byte has been the most common word length for a relatively long time in the computing world, and many of the common microprocessors that you may have heard of, such as the Z-80 and 6502 microprocessors, use the 8-bit standard. Many newer computers use the 8088, M68000, or other central processing units, which combine two bytes to form a 16-bit *word*.

Why is all this important? For one thing, these factors determine the speed of the CPU. Inside the computer, data travels from chip to chip on a set of connections called the *data bus*. In the older 8-bit systems, 8-bit bytes went zipping around on a data bus that would allow all eight bits to travel concurrently and in parallel. If more than eight bits of data were needed, however, it was necessary to wait until the bus was clear before another byte could be sent.

In some 16-bit, or 32-bit systems, 16 bits of data or 32 bits of data can be transferred in parallel at one time. The IBM PC AT and the Apple Macintosh, for example, use 16-bit data buses. This obviously means an enormous increase in speed. Unfortunately, however, the now very popular 8088 (used in the IBM PC and "work-alikes") CPU maintained the old 8-bit data bus. It is for that reason that the 8088 is sometimes referred to as an 8/16-bit microprocessor. Thus the 8088 is faster than the older systems when it performs some operations, but not when it communicates information.

The addressing capability is the other major characteristic determined by these factors. Most CPU's can take two of their words and combine them to form numbers that are larger than the numbers formed by a single word. Remember that an eight-bit byte can be used to construct a (decimal) number up to 255. When a CPU such as the Z-80 combines two such words together, however, it can construct and use a number equal to 65,535—a total of 65,536 different numbers beginning with 0. That decimal number of 65,535 then represents the largest amount of memory that can be directly accessed (in terms of numbers of bytes) or the largest number of records that can be directly accessed. We will describe how this is accomplished in our discussion of memory.

The numbers used for addressing employ another bus, called the *address bus*. The address bus in the older 8080s and Z-80s used 16 bits,

Decimal	ASCII	Binary		Decimal	ASCII	Binary
0	NUL	0000 0000		32	SP	0010 0000
1	SOH	0000 0001		33	!	0010 0001
2	STX	0000 0010		34	"	0010 0010
3	ETX	0000 0011		35	#	0010 0011
4	EOT	0000 0100		36	$	0010 0100
5	ENQ	0000 0101		37	%	0010 0101
6	ACK	0000 0110		38	&	0010 0110
7	BEL	0000 0111		39	'	0010 0111
8	BS	0000 1000		40	(	0010 1000
9	HT	0000 1001		41	)	0010 1001
10	LF	0000 1010		42	*	0010 1010
11	VT	0000 1011		43	+	0010 1011
12	FF	0000 1100		44	,	0010 1100
13	CR	0000 1101		45	−	0010 1101
14	SO	0000 1110		46	.	0010 1110
15	SI	0000 1111		47	/	0010 1111
16	DLE	0001 0000		48	0	0011 0000
17	DC1	0001 0001		49	1	0011 0001
18	DC2	0001 0010		50	2	0011 0010
19	DC3	0001 0011		51	3	0011 0011
20	DC4	0001 0100		52	4	0011 0100
21	NAK	0001 0101		53	5	0011 0101
22	SYN	0001 0110		54	6	0011 0110
23	ETB	0001 0111		55	7	0011 0111
24	CAN	0001 1000		56	8	0011 1000
25	EM	0001 1001		57	9	0011 1001
26	SUB	0001 1010		58	:	0011 1010
27	ESC	0001 1011		59	;	0011 1011
28	FS	0001 1100		60	<	0011 1100
29	GS	0001 1101		61	=	0011 1101
30	RS	0001 1110		62	>	0011 1110
31	US	0001 1111		63	?	0011 1111

Control Characters:

NUL	Null	BS	Backspace
SOH	Start of Heading	HT	Horizontal Tabulation
STX	Start of Text	LF	Line Feed
ETX	End of Text	VT	Vertical Tabulation
EOT	End of Transmission	FF	Form Feed
ENQ	Enquiry	CR	Carriage Return
ACK	Acknowledge	SO	Shift Out
BEL	Bell	SI	Shift In

35

Figure 1.1: American Standard Code for Information Interchange (ASCII) with Its Decimal and Binary Equivalents

Decimal	ASCII	Binary	Decimal	ASCII	Binary
64	@	0100 0000	96	'	0110 0000
65	A	0100 0001	97	a	0110 0001
66	B	0100 0010	98	b	0110 0010
67	C	0100 0011	99	c	0110 0011
68	D	0100 0100	100	d	0110 0100
69	E	0100 0101	101	e	0110 0101
70	F	0100 0110	102	f	0110 0110
71	G	0100 0111	103	g	0110 0111
72	H	0100 1000	104	h	0110 1000
73	I	0100 1001	105	i	0110 1001
74	J	0100 1010	106	j	0110 1010
75	K	0100 1011	107	k	0110 1011
76	L	0100 1100	108	l	0110 1100
77	M	0100 1101	109	m	0110 1101
78	N	0100 1110	110	n	0110 1110
79	O	0100 1111	111	o	0110 1111
80	P	0101 0000	112	p	0111 0000
81	Q	0101 0001	113	q	0111 0001
82	R	0101 0010	114	r	0111 0010
83	S	0101 0011	115	s	0111 0011
84	T	0101 0100	116	t	0111 0100
85	U	0101 0101	117	u	0111 0101
86	V	0101 0110	118	v	0111 0110
87	W	0101 0111	119	w	0111 0111
88	X	0101 1000	120	x	0111 1000
89	Y	0101 1001	121	y	0111 1001
90	Z	0101 1010	122	z	0111 1010
91	[	0101 1011	123	{	0111 1011
92	/	0101 1100	124	|	0111 1100
93	]	0101 1101	125	}	0111 1101
94	^	0101 1110	126	~	0111 1110
95	_	0101 1111	127	DEL	0111 1111

Control Characters:

DLE	Data Link Escape	EM	End of Medium
DC1	Device Control 1	SUB	Substitute
DC2	Device Control 2	ESC	Escape
DC3	Device Control 3	FS	File Separator
DC4	Device Control 4	GS	Group Separator
NAK	Negative Acknowledge	RS	Record Separator
SYN	Synchronous Idle	US	Unit Separator
ETB	End of Transmission Block	DEL	Delete
CAN	Cancel	SP	Space

Figure 1.1 Continued

although newer systems, such as the 8088, use a 20-bit address bus. The 20-bit system allows the direct addressing of 1,048,576 bytes (or records, or whatever). Note that the 8088 does not combine two sixteen-bit words together, as do some other systems, to form 32-bit numbers. The IBM PC AT can address memory as though it has both a 16-bit and a 32-bit address bus, but the Apple Macintosh uses only the 32-bit address bus.

Some of the more popular 8-bit micros are the Apple II family, Radio Shack Models I, II, III, and IV, the Osborne I and Executive, and the Kaypro. There are dozens of others. Apples and other 8-bit computers sold widely for home and educational use—such as the Atari 400 and 800 and the Commodore 64 and VIC 20—are based on the 6502 CPU, though most 8-bit machines sold for business use are based on the Z-80 central processing unit.

The popular 16-bit microcomputers, using the 8088, that are on the market today include the Texas Instruments Professional Computer, the IBM Personal Computer, the DEC Rainbow, the Zenith 150, the Compaq, the Columbia, and many others. The 8088 is itself a member of a family of processors that include the 8086 and the newer 80186 (and other) microprocessors. The Tandy 2000 microcomputer uses the 80186, a "true" 16-bit machine, which will run 8088 and 8086 programs.

There are more powerful 16-bit processors on the market as well, including the Motorola M68000 CPU family. The Motorola M68000, however, is a bit different from the 8088, and is often referred to as a 16/32-bit microprocessor because it uses a true 16-bit data bus and can combine two 16-bit words in order to form a 32-bit address space. It is used in the Apple Macintosh line, the Tandy (Radio Shack) Model 6000, and a growing number of others. Other examples of 16/32-bit microprocessors are the Zilog Z-8000 and the Intel 80286 CPU used in the IBM PC AT. There are others coming on the market.

In order to improve the speed and accuracy of computations of various sorts, many contemporary microcomputers now provide as an option a second CPU called a co-processor. One co-processor for the 8088-compatible family is an Intel 8087. The 8087 numeric co-processor is a new option that can make a micro run up to 100 times faster with increased accuracy in calculation-intensive applications. Such an option is particularly valuable for scientific, engineering, and other research applications requiring a large number of numeric calculations. There are co-processors available for some machines—notably the Z-80 for the Apple II series—that allow them to run additional software or other operating systems.

HOW DOES A MICROCOMPUTER REMEMBER INFORMATION?

For modern microcomputers there are essentially two primary storage options. There is the choice between electronic memory, which is an intrinsic part of the system itself, and magnetic or optical disks, which are external storage devices. Some micros still have the ability to use cassette tapes, although these are becoming rarer in the professional marketplace (except as devices that back up disk media). Electronic memory provides high-speed electronic information storage. Almost everything that a microprocessor does requires the use of some memory, and if the application is significant it may require a large amount of memory. The common buzz words are random access memory (RAM), and read only memory (ROM). Random access memory is used by the CPU for reading and writing information as it is needed by the microprocessor. It is the primary central storage for a microcomputer.

Read only memory has data loaded only once, through the use of special equipment (usually by a microcomputer manufacturer). It can be programmed so that it retains whatever is initially written to it; one cannot inadvertently erase the information contained in read only memory. ROM is used for storing basic information that is needed by the CPU every time the machine is turned on. It is also sometimes used to store commonly used applications programs for specific and dedicated purposes.

How much memory can a microcomputer have? The answer to that question is neither straightforward nor simple. First, it must be understood that memory is usually measured in units of 1024 (2^{10}) eight-bit bytes called "K," for kilobyte. Current 8088-based machines are configured with 64K to 768K bytes of RAM (although the 8088 can actually address something over one million bytes, any combination of RAM and ROM must be taken into account). On the older eight-bit machines the maximum amount of memory that could be directly addressed was 64K. And 64K was normally the maximum amount of memory that was placed on the eight-bit machines.

Memory is made available to the CPU through the address bus. Each byte in the memory is assigned an address ranging from zero to the largest address accessible by the machine. For eight-bit machines, this top address would be 65,535. The CPU keeps track of the instructions it is executing through these addresses. Programming languages can give you the capability to manipulate memory directly through these addresses as well. The POKE statement in MS-BASIC, for example, allows you to write a byte into a specific memory address; the PEEK statement allows you to display the contents of a memory address.

You might ask why all this memory is required. The answer, in short, is that many of the powerful new applications being produced for microcomputers require large amounts of memory to operate efficiently and effectively. Those applications in which the PC is used in conjunction with a large centralized mainframe system may require sufficiently sophisticated and large-scale programming that large amounts of memory are necessary. Although many sophisticated applications can be written in 64K or even less memory, some large-scale programs cannot be confined within the 64K limitation. It is probably a false economy to equip a modern microcomputer, for research use, with less than 256K of random access memory; for many emerging applications 512K or 768K will be either desirable or required.

EXTERNAL STORAGE MEDIA

If RAM and ROM memory can be referred to as internal storage media because of their close relationship to the functioning of the CPU, other devices that store information might be referred to as external storage media. The two types of storage devices are also handled differently by the CPU and by programmers using the CPU. RAM and ROM memory can be accessed directly by the CPU. Virtually every CPU has instructions that allow it or its programmer to directly transfer information from one memory location to another. With external storage devices, it is typically necessary to send information through a doorway or gateway called a *port*. The use of ports is slower than direct memory addressing and therefore limits the speed at which data can be processed. If we are willing to sacrifice some speed, we can essentially build up a system that will allow us to access a virtually unlimited amount of external storage space.

There are three primary types of external storage media available in the mid-1980s. The most popular method for storing large amounts of information are magnetic media: "floppy" flexible disks or diskettes, "hard" Winchester disks, and magnetic tape storage. As of this writing, most major microcomputers can use both floppy flexible disks and hard Winchester disks as their external storage devices. Other manufacturers of microcomputer systems are using a form of memory, called bubble memory, that can function like disks. During the mid to late-80s optical media in the form of laser video disks will become important in the microcomputer world.

Floppy disks come in several sizes. The original version of the floppy disk was 8 inches in diameter. It consisted of a disk with a magnetic coating on it, encased in a square envelope to protect it. There are still many microcomputer systems that use the 8-inch floppy diskette. The 8-inch floppies can also be seen in use with a number of major mainframe computer systems. The more common floppy disk format on microcomputers today, however, is a 5.25-inch "minifloppy." Now making its presence felt in the microcomputer market is a new, even smaller, class of not quite floppy diskettes that are 3- to 3 1/2-inches in diameter. These smaller diskettes, sometimes called "microfloppies," are actually contained in a rigid plastic case in order to protect the diskette. Although there is little standardization in the magnetic formatting of the diskettes used by various microcomputers, the new microfloppies are not yet standardized even to physical size. Nevertheless, the adoption of the Sony standard on Apple's Macintosh may solidify the microfloppy's place in the market.

Regardless of the actual physical size of the diskette, the way in which the diskettes are organized is similar but *not* standard, from one manufacturer to another. Each disk is organized into a number of *tracks,* and the tracks are subdivided into *sectors.* The track and sector organization of the disk allows data to be found by the microprocessor. Data can be recorded on disks in varying ways, the most common of which are in single or double density formats. The difference between single and double density is in the timing that takes place when data are written onto the disk medium itself. Older single density drives did not require the precision that newer double density or extended density drives require. Most contemporary drives allow the use of both single and double density formatting.

The magnetic media alternatives to floppies are hard disk drives. The hard disk drives, sometimes called Winchester drives, use a usually nonremovable rigid drive that rotates at a much higher speed than does a floppy. Winchester drives have very high capacity and a very high access speed. The initial cost of a Winchester drive can be quite high, but the actual cost per byte of storage is quite inexpensive. Winchester disk drives always are sealed. This allows the mechanical aspects of the drive to operate with greater precision. The common sizes found in microcomputers generally provide 5, 10, 15, 20, and 40 "megabytes" of storage. One megabyte is about one million (1024^2) bytes or characters of information.

Relatively new on the market today are removable cartridge hard disk drives that have some of the advantages of both the floppies and the Winchester drives. The hard disk technology allows for greater speed and precision and removability allows for essentially unlimited capacity. Removability, however, does introduce the potential for greater numbers of mechanical failures.

OTHER OLD AND NEW MEDIA

One interesting supplement to disk drives is what has come to be called RAM "disk" operating storage. In this scheme of things, part of random access memory is configured to look like a disk drive to the operating system. The advantage of using some RAM to look like a disk is that frequently used programs or data can be moved to such a RAM disk with the result that access and execution speeds are extremely fast. A disadvantage, of course, is that one must remember not to turn the machine off unless what is in the RAM disk has already been stored to a magnetic disk, because when power goes off, the RAM disk goes away, unless it is backed up by batteries, a feature that is sometimes provided with RAM disk systems.

The medium with the greatest potential for large-scale external storage in the middle to late-80s will be video laser disk technology. The primary advantage over traditional magnetic media is its very, very high capacity—in the order of 1 to 10 gigabytes. A gigabyte is about one billion (1024^3) bytes or characters of information. If we take the conservative figure of one gigabyte disk storage capacity on a standard 12-inch laser disk, we are talking about the ability to store something like the equivalent of 1500 300-page books. The disadvantage of laser disk technology until recently was that it was a read-only technology: microcomputers could read information from the disk, but could not write any new data on it. New advances in laser technology, however, have demonstrated the feasibility of both a read and write capacity. With the ability both to read and write laser disks, it should not be long before this technology becomes available as a high-density, relatively low-cost medium for computer systems of all sizes.

Several different kinds of optical laser disks will be available and in general use with microcomputers in the late 1980s: read-only disks, read-write-once disks, and read/write disks. The capacity of these laser disks is immense. The Japanese have been especially active in the development of laser disk technology, although a number of U.S. firms are in the race as well. A so-called optical read-only memory (OROM) uses a 4.72-inch disk and can contain as much as 550 megabytes of information. A standard 12-inch disk will contain huge amounts of information. For reference purposes we might note that one of the widely used magnetic disks on large IBM mainframe systems in the early to mid 1980s is the 3350 disk drive, which contained 317.5 megabytes and cost tens of thousands of dollars. The new laser disk systems will cost from a few hundred dollars to $2,000 or less; the disks themselves (removable, unlike the fixed Winchester drives) may sell for about $60. Huge databases can be distributed easily and cheaply and interactive encyclopedias are quite feasible. A survey (such as parts of the United States Census, for example) with 200,000 respondents and 5,000 characters of information on each respondent, could be recorded on a one gigabyte disk.

Microcomputer Operating Systems

Machines must have operators, organizations must have managers, and computers must have *operating systems* if they are to accomplish the work they were intended to. The most nontechnical user of a computer—even a friendly, personal microcomputer—must come to terms with the operating system. Nevertheless, researchers who are only beginning to accept the idea that a microcomputer can improve their productivity often fail to see why they should understand its operating system. After all, it is obvious to them that, although the computer's manuals may tell them they must go through the operating system to use the programs that most help them do their work, the operating system is not one of these programs. It may not be immediately apparent that the operating system does anything except give them the "prompt" sign on the computer's screen, which informs them the computer is ready to do their bidding. It may even be that, through the assistance of some ingenious programmer, the operating system has been made "transparent"—essentially invisible, to the computer user, as it is on the Apple Macintosh, for example.

It is helpful, however, to learn about your operating system. First, it is not possible to become a secure, independent, confident microcomputer user without knowing about the operating system. It is possible to be a proficient user of many application programs with only a rote knowledge of the operating system, as long as nothing ever goes wrong. But we all know that "if things can go wrong, they will." When they do go wrong, it will be unlikely that you can get them to go right again without a working knowledge of operating system procedures and programs.

Second, the operating system almost certainly has features and capabilities that will prove very useful to you, even if you have no inherent interest in how computers work. Operating systems usually include programs to erase, rename, and display the contents of disk files, to copy diskettes or files on diskettes, to set and display the date and time values stored by the computer, and to format new diskettes so they can be used. Some of these features may also be provided by the creators of application programs, but they are rarely as conveniently or powerfully implemented as they are in the operating system itself. It would be a waste of time and valuable computer resources (such as memory) to try to duplicate fully what the operating system already provides.

Finally, a good knowledge of the operating system and its features will make it possible for you to find ways to tailor your microcomputer applications to best fit your working needs. Although many researchers become fascinated with their microcomputer systems and learn to program in order to get even more out of them, others do not find learning to program to be either an interesting or cost-effective use of their time. Even if you choose never to learn to program, however, you will find that making use of some of the more advanced features of microcomputer operating systems can simplify repetitive aspects of your work and make that of less knowledgeable secretarial or clerical staff easier and more reliable.

The operating system is a computer program, but not just any computer program. It is the *controller* and *manager* of the entire computer system. All computers have operating systems. Operating systems play the same roles and provide analogous services on computers of all sizes, although the operating systems for contemporary mainframe and minicomputers are, quite naturally, much larger and more complex than microcomputer operating systems.

Those roles and services have to do with the operating system's job, management of the computer's resources. It is the operating system's job to see that information (data) gets to or from these resources in an orderly, expected, and expeditious manner, that the resources are ready to perform when they should be and are not overwhelmed when they are not ready, and that the user is alerted when something is not going right.

MICROCOMPUTER OPERATING SYSTEM TASKS

Operating systems perform three primary kinds of tasks:

(1) Handling input and output to and from all the computer's components.
(2) Establishing and maintaining a means for storing, retrieving, and documenting all the "files" of data in use on the computer.
(3) Loading and executing user or "applications" programs— programs designed to accomplish whatever work you need the computer to do.

The first task, handling input and output, is essentially a communications task. The operating system provides a means of interpreting, sending, and receiving messages:

- between the user and the display;
- between the CPU and memory;
- between the CPU and mass storage devices such as disk drives;
- between the CPU and permanent copy output devices such as printers and plotters;
- between the CPU and devices for communication with other, external computers.

Properly configured, the operating system takes care of the special electronic requirements of each of the above kinds of communication. You need to know only how to issue a command; the operating system determines what communications are necessary to accomplish the task and sees to it that the communications take place.

The second task, handling files, is essentially a directory and indexing job. Serious use of a computer requires that somebody keep track of the names, types, sizes, and locations of a large number of files of information created by and for you in the process of completing your work. The operating system takes care of this. A good operating system takes care of it so well that you need only the absolute minimum amount of information—typically a file name—to use whatever files you need, provided the file is within the operating system's purview.

If the operating system did not perform these file-handling tasks, you would be left in the same position you would be in if you tried to use a library that failed to maintain any kind of card catalog or other indexing tools. You would be required to keep—and keep track of!—your own sets of information concerning the exact location of the files (books) you needed to use. It could be done, at least if the amount of information you needed to use was limited and not mixed in with that of many other users, but it would detract seriously from the work you needed to accomplish using the files.

The third task, loading and executing application programs, is ordinarily the most important thing a researcher expects a micro-computer to do. The operating system makes it unnecessary for you to do more than ask that it be done. Without the operating system, you would need to be very concerned with the technical details of the requirements of each applications program and how these requirements could best be met by your microcomputer.

Several operating systems available for micros are examples of generic or "transportable" systems; operating systems that can be relatively easily adapted to the hardware of the computers produced by more than one manufacturer. The use of such systems has become the de facto standard since the development of CP/M for 8-bit microcomputers in the late 1970s. They have supplanted or, in some cases, supplemented the alternative: manufacturer-specific operating systems such as those produced by Apple Computer, Radio Shack, and Commodore. With the 16-bit systems, such as the IBM PC or the Tandy 2000, MS-DOS (called PC-DOS by IBM) from Microsoft has become the standard; in the future, UNIX from AT&T may be the major standard. Most 16-bit computers are capable of running several different operating systems without modification to the machine's hardware; however, the older 8-bit systems such as the Apple II series require significant modification. For a good series of articles on operating systems in general and the factors that should affect your choice of one, see Allswang (1983a, 1983b) and Heintz (1983b).

The Compatibility Problem

Now that we have introduced some basic computer concepts, we are ready for a discussion of a problem that micro users and those thinking of buying microcomputers must confront: Will the program I want run on this (or my) particular computer? Several factors influence the answer to this question.

First, a program that is written on a computer with a particular CPU—the 6502 for instance—will not run without modification on another CPU, like the 8088 or the M68000. Apple II programs will not run on the IBM PC, nor will they run on the Apple Macintosh. Commercial software developers spend a significant amount of their time writing conversions of programs from one CPU to another, but these conversions, although appearing the same to the user, may be dramatically different from the original. If a version of the program you want is available for your computer, these differences may not be important to you. If a version is not available, the difficulty of the conversion may deter the software developer from writing one.

Generally speaking, programs written for one CPU in a family, like the 8086-8088-80186 CPUs, are fairly easily transportable to other family members. Some programs will require no conversion at all. Some computer manufacturers who use the same CPU use different operating systems, however, and thus their programs are not compatible. The Commodore 64 and Apple II are examples, as both use the 6502 CPU but different operating systems. This kind of conversion problem is not so formidable, and you will find that software vendors often sell versions of their programs for several computers in the same CPU family.

Even computers with the same operating systems and the same CPUs may be incompatible, however. Some manufacturers, IBM being the notable example, include proprietary ROM in their machines, which contains instructions specific to that computer. If a program author uses some of these instructions in his or her program, the program will only work on that manufacturer's machine. Some manufacturers use different disk formats than others, so programs written with their disk formats may not be read by other manufacturer's disk drives.

Another level of compatibility is *data* compatibility. Micros with the same or similar CPUs that are running the same operating system can often read each other's disks if the disks contain only data—text from a word processing program or numeric data for statistical analysis, for example. They may be able to do this even though they cannot run the same version of the word processor or statistical program that created the data. This means that researchers can exchange data and text regardless of whether they have the same computer or can run the same programs, as long as the machines are data compatible.

The IBM PC can read data disks created on the Texas Instruments Professional, for instance, because they share the same operating system—MS-DOS—and the same CPU—the 8088. The Tandy 2000, with its 80186 CPU, can read disks created by either the IBM or the Texas Instruments PC, but these machines cannot read Tandy 2000 disks unless the Tandy creates them with a special compatible format.

The compatibility problem has several important effects for the microcomputer owner or buyer. It causes the micro market to be dominated by the machines from one or two vendors. Software developers write programs for these machines first, the availability of software stimulates the sales of these machines, the sales encourage the developers to write more programs, which sells more machines, and so on. This domination begins by a combination of luck, timing, and the vagaries of capitalism, and has almost nothing to do with the technological sophistication or quality of the machines involved. The Apple II, the former industry giant, and the IBM PC, the current leader, are in many ways inferior to their competitors. This means nothing, however, if the program you and thousands of others want is not available on a superior computer.

The compatibility problem is thus important when buying a microcomputer or micro software. You must make sure that the machine and the programs match. If you want a particular computer, you must ensure that the software you want is available for it, or that you can live with the programs that will run on it. If you have a particular program in mind, you have to get a computer that will make it work.

Conclusion

Researchers cannot avoid the microcomputer nor should they wish to. The microcomputer is revolutionizing the way in which we do computing, and research activities will have to confront that revolution. The time it takes to prepare, execute, analyze, and publish new research is being compressed by the new tools available. In the remaining pages of this book we will attempt to detail the opportunities available and how to use them in the research enterprise.

For Further Reading

For an introduction to microcomputers in general and to their uses in educational and research settings, you should consult Schrodt (1984). A good way to begin a study of the topics discussed in this chapter is with a volume that presents an overall approach to using microcomputers to improve the productivity of professionals, an occupational class that certainly includes researchers. One that we can highly recommend is *Your T.I. Professional Computer: Use, Applications and BASIC* (Madron and Tate, 1984), which is much more about the uses of micros by professionals than it is about the particular computer it employs to illustrate those uses. In any case, the TIPC is an example of the most popular class of business and professional microcomputers in the mid-1980's, those based on CPU chips in the Intel 8088/8086/80186 family, which also includes the IBM-PC, DEC Rainbow, AT&T 6300, Compaq, Columbia, Eagle, HP-150, Seequa Chamelion, and dozens of others.

Other excellent sources of information about microcomputers are the magazines devoted to the topic. The oldest is *Creative Computing,* which is often very useful. It concentrates on the use of micros in education and the home. Probably the most well known are *BYTE* and *Infoworld.* All of these magazines routinely print reviews and product evaluations in a broad range of areas of interest to microcomputer owners. Articles on programming techniques are also popular in *Creative Computing* and *BYTE.* The advertising in all three journals is informative, being addressed primarily to knowledgeable micro users.

2. WRITING THE RESEARCH PROPOSAL

The first and most important use you are likely to make of a microcomputer is word processing. In this section, we consider how microcomputer word processing can help you get through what is often one of the most difficult stages of a research project: writing the research proposal. Later we shall consider how word processing and related microcomputer text processing programs can assist you in writing the research report.

Word Processing for Proposal Preparation

Sometime in their careers most researchers find it necessary to learn to type—even if badly—in order to conduct their work effectively. Many who do and all who do not remain dependent upon the help of a typist to prepare final drafts of their documents. Experienced researchers recognize the tensions and sleepless nights brought on by the struggle to complete a research project proposal in time to make a deadline. The struggle is made all the more difficult by the necessity to leave enough time for the typist to prepare the final draft of the proposal. Word processing can clearly gain valuable time for you in several ways.

Many researchers are well aware that word processing can ease the preparation of the written documents they must constantly produce. Not all, however, recognize why this is so. A few words on the advantages of word processing may thus be in order. First, if microcomputer word processing won't make a good typist out of a bad one, it will greatly relieve the drudgery of correction that makes the labor of a poor typist so debilitating and unproductive, and the product of that labor less legible for whoever must prepare the final draft. This is true to such an extent that poor typists find typing less burdensome. Consequently, they type more of their work, thereby improving their skills.

The result often is that many researchers come to find the labor involved in marking corrections on paper drafts and making editing explanations to a competent typist takes more time than editing and correcting their own rough work to produce a final copy. As a bonus, the time formerly required to get the manuscript retyped by a secretary is saved.

If you don't type, or if you have good, prompt secretarial assistance and leave plenty of time before deadlines, you may not find the argument of the preceding paragraphs compelling. Even so, word processing can be of significant benefit by improving the productivity of the secretary who prepares your research proposals. Estimates vary, but all authorities agree that word processing improves secretarial productivity by 30% or more, because, at a minimum, it eliminates retyping of correct text and makes correction of errors so much easier than it is when typewriter and paper are used. Quite simply, this means that, even if the time required for the typist to produce the proposal can't be eliminated, it can be reduced substantially. More time is made available for creative activities.

Given a tight proposal deadline, the reduction of the time required to produce a final draft of a proposal made possible by microcomputer word processing may be very important indeed. But in our view, it may be the least important of the increases in personal or secretarial productivity and effectiveness that word processing can contribute to the proposal preparation process. Word processing not only simplifies drafting proposals, it encourages redrafting that makes proposals clearer and more effective; makes it simple to create, insert, and alter the frequently-used text that is essential to most proposals; and greatly eases reformatting of proposals for alternative submissions, or in the event of a rejection, for modification and resubmission.

Text Editors and Text Formatters

A wide variety of word processing systems exist. Even leaving aside two major varieties of word processing—dedicated word processors and mainframe/minicomputer word processing facilities—the range of microcomputer programs that can justifiably be called word processors is mind boggling. Nevertheless, all word processing systems, regardless of the machinery on which they run, have two basic components: a *text editor* and a *text formatter*. The text editor allows the quick and easy entry, correction, editing, and manipulation of words (text), regardless of how those words might look if printed. The text formatter prints a document produced by the text editor in the form and with the appearance you specify.

Historically, there have been two varieties of text editors: line editors and full-screen editors. Microcomputer line editors emerged at the beginning of microcomputing, when it was not at all certain that a computer user had a cathode ray tube (CRT) terminal on which a full screen of information could be displayed all at once, even if the editor was capable of generating one. Because line editors display and edit only one line of text at a time, as their name implies, they were suitable for use on the slow-printing terminals such as teletypes that were usually available to users.

Full-screen editors display a full screen of text at a time and allow movement of the computer's cursor (the marker that indicates your place on the screen) easily to any place on the screen to enter text or make changes. Full-screen editors for micros arrived later than line editors.

There are many line editors still available for microcomputers today; usually, one comes with the operating system for the computer. There are many others in the public software domain. Nevertheless, the most popular word processors for microcomputers provide full-screen editors of greater or lesser sophistication, and we shall generally assume in what follows that you, as a researcher learning or wishing to use a microcomputer, have access to full screen editing.

Like text editors, text formatters also come in two varieties: *command-driven* and *on-screen* ("what you see is what you get") formatters. Command-driven formatters require you to enter, along with your text, explicit commands that control the appearance the text will have when it is printed out. For example, you might enter ".11 65" to establish a line length of 65 characters, ".pa" to force a page break, ".sk 3" to force a skip of 3 lines, and ".ds" to print the text double-spaced. The formatting commands have no effect on the appearance of the text on-screen. A command-driven formatter may be combined with a text editor, either a line or full-screen editor. But this is not necessary; it may be able to work with text prepared by any text editor.

"What you see is what you get" formatters attempt to display text on a CRT exactly as it will appear when printed out, within the limits imposed by the display screen. You accomplish this by entering formatting commands that take effect immediately. On-screen formatters are necessarily combined with full-screen editors—it would not be possible to show and alter how the text will appear otherwise.

Like line editors, command-driven text formatters were created to provide word processing functions when users might not have video terminals on which they could view how their text would look when printed out. Although line editors appear to most computer users to be clearly inferior to full-screen editors, the command-driven text formatters are not necessarily inferior to "what you see is what you get" formatters, especially for the preparation of relatively long documents such as research proposals and papers.

Despite the ingenuity of their programmers, the limitations of most microcomputer display screens make it cumbersome or even impossible for on-screen formatters to show some kinds of text as it will appear when printed. To take only the most obvious case, the standard 40-column displays of unaugmented Apple IIs, Commodore 64s, and similar machines, or the 64-column standard display of Radio Shack Models I, III, and IV cannot show even a full line of text as it would appear when printed on a standard 8½" by 11" sheet of paper with 1" margins. Even computers that display 80 characters of text across a line do not usually show more than 23 lines at a time.

Furthermore, it is generally easier to reformat an existing text file with a command-driven formatter. To do so, you need only change a few formatting commands that affect the entire file. With an on-screen formatter, you may have to reformat the entire file painstakingly, one paragraph at a time. As a consequence, the following points are true:

- both command-driven and on-screen formatters are popular in contemporary microcomputer word processing systems;

- full-screen text editors provided with many command-driven formatters often make a serious attempt to show text on-screen as it will appear on printout; and
- "what you see is what you get" formatters may also provide a set of formatting commands that do not affect the on-screen text display, but provide alternative formatting on printout, if used.

Drafting and Redrafting with a Word Processor

Many research proposals fail because they are unclear or simply poorly drafted. Microcomputers and their word processing programs can't solve this problem. But because they make drafting, redrafting, and rearrangement of their electronic text so easy, they can help.

Drafting proposals with a good word processor encourages thoughtful writing and good style. The ease with which changes are made in the electronic document produced by a word processor emboldens writers not to be satisfied with a second-best word, to attack the awkward-appearing sentence again, to move a slightly-out-of-place sentence to where it really belongs. All this is accomplished by issuing simple commands to the word processor's text editor.

The ease of drafting with a microcomputer word processor results from the capabilities that a good word processing program will have.[1] First among these are powerful cursor controls that provide the ability to move through the text up, down, left, and right in increments of a character, word, line, paragraph, screen, or page, or to the beginning or end of the document being worked on.

To make changes in existing text, you simply move the cursor to where the changes should begin and start typing. You will be aided by a second important feature of the word processor: the ability to delete a character, word, line, paragraph, screen, or page by a simple command or set of commands (depending upon the scope of the deletion you wish to make), to delete text by typing new text over it, or to insert new text amounting to a character, word, line, paragraph, screen, page, or even a whole separate file exactly where you want it. Reformatting changed text using the text editor's on-screen reformatting commands or inserting the commands to insure proper reformatting on output by the word processor's command-driven text formatter, as appropriate, will ensure that the changed text has the proper appearance, regardless of how muddled it may have gotten in the interim.

The word processor's ability to mark and move around or copy segments (blocks) of text ranging in size from a character to a page or more allows a proposal author to put text where it belongs, rather than (or in addition to) where it was typed in. Finally, the word processor's ability to find and change segments of text throughout the whole document (globally), if desired, with as much or as little author control over changes as desired, provides a most powerful way of fixing persistent errors (misspellings, incorrect names or numbers, etc.) or painlessly implementing changes of mind.

Another set of word processor capabilities eases the drudgery associated with making sure a document has the proper appearance when completed. Microcomputer word processors can

- automatically center text on command;
- print text (and perhaps show it on-screen) with an even or ragged right margin, as desired;
- begin a new line automatically when the right margin is reached without striking the carriage return, and without breaking a word;
- set new margins and spacing easily and as often as desired with a minimum of effort on your part;
- automatically put the proper number of lines of text on a page with no attention or intervention by you;
- set automatic "headers" or "footers" to be printed on each page, and include accurate page numbers, if desired;
- keep track on-screen of the page of text currently being viewed as well as the line and column position of the cursor on the page;
- indicate on-screen where each page breaks given current margins and spacing;
- automatically handle the placement of footnotes where they should go: the bottom of a page, end of the document, or wherever.

The final appearance of proposals prepared on a word processor can be enhanced easily as you prepare the proposal draft by the use of "print fonts" or other print enhancements provided by the program. Microcomputer word processors generally provide easy ways to indicate that text should be underlined or printed in italics, bold faced, superscripted, subscripted, printed at different pitches, proportionally spaced, or printed with an "overstrike" character superimposed on each text character, provided the printer attached to the computer can do these things. Although only a few of these print enhancements—true boldfacing, for example—cannot be accomplished on a typewriter, those that can be done usually require the expenditure of a significantly greater amount of labor.

All these features of microcomputer word processors make the laborious task of drafting a research proposal easier and more efficient. Nevertheless, drafting is still dependent mostly upon the quality and effort of the human mind working the keyboard.

By comparison, redrafting can be a mostly mechanical task of integrating acceptable changes suggested by co-authors, editors, proofreaders, or the original author once the first draft has been completed and reread. Here word processors really shine. First, they make the correcting of "that which has been incorrectly typed" much easier. Second, they make possible the practical implementation of a principle that poor typists and proofreaders no doubt think should have been natural law: "that which has been correctly typed once, shall never be retyped." You (or your typist) need no longer dread the insertion of the omitted phrase or suggested new paragraph that will cause this page to spill over to the next, that page to spill over to the next, and so on in a textual domino effect that mandates retyping pages of correct text. Retyping becomes reprinting, ordinarily at a pace far more rapid than that achieved by the best typist, when the word processor is instructed to print the redrafted document.

Outline Processors and Proposal Preparation

Recently, a variety of microcomputer text processing software has been created that can go even further in improving the quality and ease of preparation of research proposals. Labeled "Outline" or "Idea Processors," such programs as ThinkTank, Framework, or FREE-STYLE allow a researcher to create an outline and text to go with that outline almost in stream-of consciousness fashion, but with an organizing structure that greatly facilitates the restructuring of the outline and text. Some idea processors (FREESTYLE, for example) automatically rearrange text when the structure of its outline is rearranged. Using an idea processor, the drafting of a proposal or report can be well along before its conceptualization and outlining is finished.

Word Processing and Multiple Authors

The use of a word processor also facilitates communication between co-authors. At the very least, successive drafts of a proposal can be delivered on diskettes, and each author can edit the text on his or her own microcomputer. A more rapid means of communication, particularly for co-authors at different institutions, would be the electronic communication of drafts from micro to micro, using communications software and hardware discussed below.

These sorts of arrangements work best, of course, when all the authors use the same or similar types of microcomputers. The most critical determinant of compatibility, however, is the word processing software. Different word processing programs that run on the same computer will often store the text in formats that are incompatible. Command-driven formatters will not recognize the text generated by on-screen formatting programs, two different command-driven programs will use different commands, and one on-screen formatter will not read the output of another. Four different brands of microcomputers were used in the preparation of this book, but we limited ourselves to one word processing program, WordStar.

The way in which the word processing program stores text may have other implications. WordStar, for example, uses the eighth bit in a byte to store formatting information. Not only does this practice make WordStar text unreadable by many other word processors, it also hampers electronic communication of the text, because communications programs often use the eighth bit for parity checking.

Using "Boiler Plate"

Researchers who prepare more than one research proposal find that very different proposals frequently require the inclusion of "boiler plate" text—more or less standard text that changes little from document to document. For example, many proposal outlines require that information about the university or research agency sponsoring the research be provided and that your curriculum vitae and those of any other investigators associated with the project be included. If this information could literally be presented in an identical format each time it was required, you could simply reproduce a master copy in the requisite number of copies and staple them to the research proposal. Unfortunately, that is not how it works. The exact format in which the information is required will probably vary from proposal outline to proposal outline. Furthermore, the information that must be provided does change slightly from time to time: the university's enrollment changes, you publish a new article, and so on.

In the absence of a word processor, the proposal boiler plate information must be edited and painstakingly retyped when each new proposal is prepared. With a word processor, the boiler plate can be entered once and stored on diskettes for editing and reuse as necessary. Once in the document, it can be edited to make necessary changes, rearranged to fit more consistently into the style of the current document, or reformatted.

Reformatting for
Alternative Submissions

Adequate funding for a research project is not, by all appearances, a civil right of researchers. To the contrary, securing it can require perseverance. Competition for research funds can be so great that even the best proposal may objectively have a much less than even chance of securing any funding. Another proposal may require funding from two or more sources to be successful. Consequently, researchers always face the necessity of submitting a proposal more than once to ensure that it has more than one chance in a competitive grant market, to secure the necessary funds from more than one agency, or, sadly, to resubmit a good proposal that failed the first time around.

Preparing alternative versions of the same proposal for submission to different grantors is another area in which a word processor can make you more effective and productive. An entire proposal can be treated like the boiler plate material discussed above. It can be copied to a new file for the alternative submission in which it can be edited extensively and rearranged as necessary. New material required by the different grantor can be inserted, unnecessary material may be excised, and the emphasis or focus of the proposal can be changed if necessary. All this can be done to the electronic text far more quickly and easily than it could be to paper drafts. And, when the necessary changes are done, the word processor will print out the new proposal in exactly the format required by the new grantor in a fraction of the time it would require to type a final draft by hand.

A Comparison of Six Word Processing Programs

Figure 2.1 compares the features of six of the most popular word processing programs for microcomputers: WordStar, Microsoft Word, Multimate, pfs:Write, Apple Writer, and MacWrite. WordStar, Microsoft Word, Multimate, and pfs:Write are available for the IBM PC and most other micros that can run the MS-DOS operating system.

	WordStar	Microsoft Word	Multi-mate	pfs: Write	Apple-writer	MacWrite
Computers:	IBM Apple II CP/M	IBM	IBM	IBM Apple II	Apple II	Macin-tosh
Minimum Memory:	64K	128K	256K	64K	64K	128K
Retail Price:	$495	$375	$495	$140	$195	$99
Merge files:	yes	yes	yes	no	yes	no
Super-scripts:	yes	yes	yes	no	yes	yes
On screen help:	yes	yes	yes	yes	yes	no
Split screen:	no	yes	no	no	yes	no
File size limit:	disk	disk	disk	disk	disk	*20 pp.
Automatic backup:	yes	yes	yes	yes	no	no
Mail Merge:	add on	yes	yes	add on	yes	add on
Mouse:	no	add on	no	no	no	yes

SOURCE: Updated from Lockwood (1984).
*80 pages on 512K Macintosh.

Figure 2.1:   A Comparison of Six Word Processing Programs

WordStar is also available for CP/M machines and the Apple II series, and pfs:Write has a version for Apple II computers. Apple Writer is available for the Apple II family, and MacWrite is sold for the Apple Macintosh computer.

All of these programs have full-screen editors and are more or less "what you see is what you get" formatters. They all provide full cursor movement features and the standard editing functions, including character, word and line deletes and inserts, global search and replace, and cutting and pasting operations. They all have standard formatting capabilities, including adjustable margins, right and left margin justification, centering, headers, and footers.

The figure compares the programs on ten features. The minimum memory describes the smallest memory configuration required to run the program. Pfs:Write requires 128K on the IBM PC and similar computers, but needs only 64K on the Apple II. Multimate requires the largest amount of memory, 256K on the IBM PC. The packages range widely in list retail price, from $99 for MacWrite to $495 for WordStar and Multimate. Most of these programs can be obtained for much less through mail-order discount companies who advertise in microcomputer magazines. Dealers will often offer discounts as well, and some manufacturers or dealers will include one of these word processors with the purchase of a microcomputer.

The ability to merge files is important in the preparation of many kinds of documents, particularly when using the boiler plate concepts discussed above. Not all word processors have this feature, however, as shown by pfs:Write and MacWrite in the figure. Superscripts are sometimes necessary in typing footnotes and mathematical formulae, but not every word processor has this capacity. Even when the program can accomplish this, however, the printer used to print the document must also be able to perform this function.

On-screen help is particularly useful for the novice word processor user. This function allows you to ask the program to describe or explain a particular command without leaving the document on which you are working. Again, not all word processors have this ability. The split-screen function allows you to edit two documents or two pieces of the same document simultaneously, with both parts displayed on the screen at the same time. This feature is fairly advanced, and only a minority of programs offer it.

Some word processing programs restrict the size of the document you may create. Depending on how the program is written, the size of the document may be limited by your disk capacity, the amount of memory in your micro, or some other constraint. Five of the packages limit the document to the capacity of your disk, although MacWrite constrains it to 20 pages. Because MacWrite also does not allow documents to be merged or concatenated, this limitation could be serious for researchers.

Automatic backup is a feature in which the program automatically creates a copy of your document while you are working. If something catastrophic occurs—for instance, electrical service is interrupted—the backup copy of your document is preserved so that not all of your work is lost. The alternative is for you to remember to save your work to disk periodically, something that few computer users learn to do without experiencing a disaster first hand.

Mail merging is used to create form letters and other documents in which multiple copies are required with minor changes in each copy. A file of changes is merged by the program with a second file that contains the standard part of the text. Some researchers, particularly journal editors and officers in professional associations, will find this feature invaluable. Others will never need it. For this reason, it is often sold as a separate, add-on feature to word processing programs.

A mouse is a hand-held pointing device that allows the cursor to move around on the screen by moving the mouse around on your desk or a special pad. It also has one to three keys or buttons with which you can enter simple commands. A mouse is not terribly useful for text entry, but many people find it extraordinarily handy for editing. Like mail merging, this feature is optional with some word processors.

For Further Reading

Reviews of individual word processing programs are more numerous than the programs themselves. A good general guide to word processing choices is Heintz (1982a). Also useful and very witty is McWilliams (1983). Of some value are Good (1982), Shuford (1983), and Lockwood (1984).

3. CREATING AND MANAGING THE PROPOSAL BUDGET

Probably the most onerous task you will face in writing a research proposal is the creation and management of the proposal budget. Here, however, is where you most resemble the person for whom most microcomputer software is created: the business person. Microcomputer software developers have devised dozens of so-called "spreadsheet" programs that make budgeting and accounting almost (but not quite) painless. In fact, these programs, with names like VisiCalc, Lotus 1-2-3, and Multiplan, are so successful at this task that they have become the most popular computer programs ever written.

The granddaddy of all spreadsheet programs, VisiCalc, was originally written by a Harvard Business School student as an aid in accounting, reporting, and forecasting. VisiCalc, which was described by its creator as "an electronic blackboard and electronic chalk," was such a phenomenal success in the marketplace (selling hundreds of thousands of copies), that imitators soon sprang up. Today there are about three dozen different programs of this type available, ranging in price from $30 or $40 to about $400 for a full-featured program. Lotus 1-2-3, the current champion seller, is an example of a so-called "integrated" package that combines a spreadsheet with other functions such as a database manager, a word processor, or a graphics program.

The concept behind a spreadsheet program is simple yet powerful. The program provides you with a "blackboard" on the screen composed of numbered rows and columns and a set of mathematical (and even statistical—more about that later) operations that can be applied to these rows and columns, and to the cells formed by the row and column intersections. The cursor acts as the "chalk," and can be moved around on the screen with control keys or arrow keys on the keyboard, or a mouse. Numbers and labels for the rows, columns, or cells can be entered, or defined by formulae in terms of other rows, columns, or cells. Most spreadsheet programs allow you to access many more rows and columns than are visible on the screen at any one time, and the more advanced packages allow you to define parts of the current worksheet in terms of other worksheets stored on disk.

Another advantage to spreadsheet programs is their ease of use. Spreadsheet programs have been designed to sell to business people who have little knowledge of microcomputers, and even less desire to acquire any. In consequence, popular spreadsheet programs come with elaborate tutorials, fairly readable documentation, and extensive on-line "help" facilities. In addition, third-party software developers have come up with various kinds of enhancements and instructional materials to accompany the spreadsheets. Finally, the microcomputer book market is replete with books on spreadsheet programs. All of this means that you may find spreadsheets quite a bit easier to use than other kinds of microcomputer software.

Spreadsheet Programs and Budget Preparation

Figure 3.1 shows how the screen from Multiplan, a popular spreadsheet available for Apple, CP/M, and MS-DOS micros, appears

```
#1       1         2         3         4         5         6         7
 1              January  February   March     April      May      June
 2
 3 Salaries
 4       Tom $2000.00  $2000.00                         $2000.00  $2000.00
 5      Neal $1750.00  $1750.00  $1750.00  $1750.00     $1750.00  $1750.00
 6       Bob $1675.00  $1675.00  $1675.00               $1800.00  $1800.00
 7     Sec'y $1500.00  $1500.00  $1500.00  $1500.00     $1500.00  $1500.00
 8     Inter           $5000.00  $5000.00  $5000.00
 9           --------------------------------------------------------------
10  Subtotal $6925.00 $11925.00  $9925.00  $8250.00     $7050.00  $7050.00
11
12 Expenses
13    Travel $2575.00  $1200.00                                   $3400.00
14    Phones  $200.00  $1200.00  $1200.00  $1200.00      $200.00   $200.00
15  Supplies  $500.00  $1500.00  $1500.00  $1500.00      $750.00   $500.00
16      Misc  $327.50   $390.00   $270.00   $270.00       $95.00   $410.00
17           --------------------------------------------------------------
18  Subtotal $3602.50  $4290.00  $2970.00  $2970.00     $1045.00  $4510.00
19
20
COMMAND: Alpha Blank Copy Delete Edit Format Goto Help Insert Lock Move
         Name Options Print Quit Sort Transfer Value Window Xternal
Select option or type command letter
R1C1                             87% Free       Multiplan: BUDGET
```

Figure 3.1:   An Example of a Spreadsheet (Multiplan) Screen

with some mythical data for a research project budget. This budget illustrates several features of a versatile spreadsheet program. The program keeps the row and column numbers visible on the screen so that you can locate cells easily; it keeps the "menu" of possible commands available at all times, freeing you from dependence on a manual or reference card. The bottom line of the screen displays the current cursor location (row one, column one), the amount of the spreadsheet that is unused, and the file name under which the data is stored. You can execute any of the commands shown by typing the first letter of the command name. This causes the program to display a second list of options associated with the command.

The data entered on the spreadsheet also illustrate some useful features of the program. Note, for example, that the columns can contain either words or numbers, that cell, column, or row entries can be centered, or left or right justified, and entire rows, columns, or cells can be left blank. In entering the data, it was not necessary for us to type in each cell entry by hand. The entries for the secretary's salary, for example, were generated by typing in the salary for the first month, and then telling the program that the other entries in that row were equal to the first one. Likewise, we were able to leave all the calculations to the spreadsheet program. The subtotals in row 10, for instance, were generated by defining that row as the sum of rows 4 through 8, and the row labeled "Misc" under the Expenses section was computed by taking 10 percent of rows 13 through 15.

The program calculates and prints the values of cells defined this way immediately, although you can turn this feature off if you want to. This makes updating and correcting the spreadsheet especially easy. For example, if we find that our secretary demands more money than we have allocated in the budget, say $1600 per month, we merely have to change the cell in row 7, column 2. Because the other cells in row 7, and the cells in row 10, are defined in terms of the cell we have changed, the program immediately increases all of these cells by $100. Any other cells that depend for their values on the cell we have changed, or on any of the others that have just been updated (like a grand total cell located somewhere else on the spreadsheet) will also be modified accordingly.

The more sophisticated spreadsheet programs also allow you to define cells, columns, or rows in terms of other spreadsheets. Say, for instance, that the travel expense located in row 13, column 2, is actually a total figure derived from another budget on another spreadsheet. Rather than manually copying this total from the other spreadsheet to this one, we can tell the program to get the entry for this cell directly from the other sheet, which we have previously saved to disk. Thus, if we make a change to the other sheet, in response to an increase in airline fares or some other disaster, the program will update the cell on this sheet as well, without requiring us to remember to do so.

You can see that these features make spreadsheet programs extremely valuable tools in compiling a research budget. The ability to define cells in terms of other cells or in terms of mathematical formulae, and to update quickly one or more spreadsheets in response to changes, allows us an additional benefit: we can indulge in an exercise in anxiety called "what if" forecasting. What if Tom decided to work all six months on the project, instead of only four? What if Tom, Neal, and Bob decided to work full time instead of part time? What if Neal insisted that his salary be indexed to inflation? What if the interviewers go on strike? What if miscellaneous expenses are actually 20 percent of other expenses, instead of 10 percent? All of these questions can be answered by making minor changes to a few of the cells in the spreadsheet, and our worst fears will be confirmed immediately. The key to making this type of

INTERVIEWER NAME	WAGE PER HOUR	HOURS WORKED	COMPLETED SURVEYS	SURVEYS PER HOUR	TOTAL PAY
Alan (Sprv)	$5.50	40.00	0		$220.00
Barbara	$3.65	23.25	15	0.65	$84.86
Charlotte	$3.65	15.00	10	0.67	$54.75
Darlene	$4.50	20.75	17	0.82	$93.38
Elliot	$3.65	25.00	19	0.76	$91.25
Frank	$4.75	18.25	13	0.71	$86.69
Gene	$3.65	12.25	9	0.73	$44.71
Harriet	$4.00	20.00	21	1.05	$80.00
Iris (Sprv)	$5.50	35.75	0		$196.63
Janice	$4.00	18.00	16	0.89	$72.00
Kathy	$3.65	12.50	9	0.72	$45.63
Lawrence	$4.25	16.00	16	1.00	$68.00
Monica	$3.65	17.50	13	0.74	$63.88
Nancy	$3.65	10.50	8	0.76	$38.33

TOTAL SURVEYS:	166		SALARY COSTS:	$1240.09	
COST PER SURVEY:	$7.47		AVERAGE WAGE:	$4.15	

Figure 3.2: A Multiplan Spreadsheet to Calculate Interviewer Productivity and Costs

procedure work is to define the cell entries in the spreadsheet in as generalized a way as possible, and to avoid entering numeric "constants." You can think of any constants in your spreadsheet as assumptions about a forecasting model; if you change the assumptions, then the whole model will change, given that the model is defined in terms of the constants.

Just as generating research proposals often involves the creation of "boiler plate," budgets for different projects often resemble each other in form, if not in content. Once you have saved a spreadsheet to disk, it can become a "template" for future spreadsheets that will have basically the same types of row and column labels, and the same relationships among cells, rows, and columns. These templates can be used over and over for a variety of research and other projects.

Managing the Proposal Budget

Assuming that your research proposal and its accompanying budget have now been funded, you are presented with the task of managing the budget as the project moves along. Once again, the features of a spreadsheet program can help. Figure 3.2 shows an example of the kind of data a researcher might want to collect in the course of managing a project budget.

The only data that we have entered on this spreadsheet are the wages per hour of the interviewers, the hours the interviewers worked, and the number of surveys they completed. We then asked the spreadsheet program to compute the productivity of the interviewers in terms of completed surveys per hour, the total pay the interviewers have earned, the total number of surveys collected, and the total salary costs. We also asked the program to figure out the labor cost per survey and the average wage per hour of our interviewers.

How can this information be used in managing the project budget? Obviously, keeping track of the total salary costs and the total pay for each interviewer is important. The total salary costs can be "plugged in" to a cell on another spreadsheet that summarizes other costs, and running totals of the expenses can be maintained. Similarly, we could use these totals to forecast future expenses, if we can give the spreadsheet a formula with which to generate the forecasts. The spreadsheet program gives us much more power to control the budget than this, however.

Say, for example, that the labor costs per survey are exceeding the figure we had budgeted initially. The "what if" facility that the spreadsheet provides can help us find strategies, quickly and easily, to keep these costs under control. Perhaps we should demand that the interviewer supervisors conduct a few surveys themselves. Maybe we should reward the more productive interviewers, or punish the less productive ones. We might have to let a few interviewers go. By entering a few different values into the spreadsheet, we can see the effects of these changes on productivity and costs.

In summary, then, spreadsheet programs can be very helpful tools to the researcher, especially in budget preparation and control. Spreadsheet programs are very flexible, powerful, and easy to use, especially when compared with other kinds of microcomputer software. Although some of these packages can be fairly expensive, they will often pay for themselves by saving endless hours of calculation.

For Further Reading

Three competent general spreadsheet reviews are Heintz (1982b, 1983c) and Ahl (1984). There are also entire books dedicated to the most popular spreadsheet programs, like Lotus 1-2-3 and Multiplan. See Stultz (1984) and Baras (1984) for examples.

4. DATA GATHERING

Microcomputers can be of great assistance in several phases of data-gathering for a research project. They can help make traditional pencil and paper based activities such as note-taking and organizing more effective. They can provide friendly, easy-to-use support programs for the entry of research data of a wide variety of kinds. Their word processing capabilities are ideal for drafting and formatting question-naires for surveys. For some analysts, they have already become the basis for automated survey research, from sample selection to dialing (in telephone surveys) to interview administration. The new, more powerful micros of "lap," "notebook," or smaller size that have now become available should become essential tools in research "in the field." Already in use as process controllers in the life and physical sciences, micros can also make process control in political and social experi-mental research a practicality. Finally, their communications capa-bilities allow data to be quickly and accurately transferred from field sites to headquarters, from one researcher to another, from data archives to individual researchers or research groups at remote locations, or anywhere else it may be needed, often without the involvement of a large central computer system.

Note-Taking and Organizing
with Microcomputers

One of the most traditional and important steps in any research project is taking and organizing notes. The notes may provide the entries in the project bibliography, summarize the relevant findings of the existing literature, provide the raw data on which later quantitative coding will be based, provide authority for conclusions to be asserted in the research report, and so on. Traditional methods of note-taking have involved the use of index cards on which the necessary information was entered. Cards are used so that the pieces of information can be titled and classified into categories for later organization in support of the research.

These practices have changed slightly with the advent of cheap, publicly available copy machines. It is usually no longer necessary to copy long passages from books and articles to the note cards, because the relevant portions of the research sources can be photocopied, marked, and classified. But if the sources are to be used effectively, they must be read, entered into the bibliography, and probably classified through the use of key words or phrases of some kind. Otherwise retrieval of the information in the sources for later use will be difficult or virtually impossible. Of course there will still be many sources of "notes" that are too voluminous to be photocopied and annotated; they will have to be read and summarized either for their substantive content or for the purpose of coding their content at a later time for analysis.

Microcomputers and their specialized software can certainly ease the preparation of notes if they have to be copied to some medium other than that of their source. A word processor can ease the entry of the text for notes as much as it can the preparation of the text of a research proposal or the final report. But other programs generally created for other purposes, particularly file and data base managers, can be even more handy for note-taking tasks such as indexing and data entry. Finally, special purpose microcomputer programs exist that are specifically intended for note-taking and indexing tasks.

We shall not spend much time discussing how word processors can aid note-taking and organization. Notes are text, and we have already indicated how microcomputer word processors can make the production of text more efficient and less painful. Suffice it to say that the existence of a word processor is taken for granted by a number of programs that are most useful in note-taking and organization tasks. Useful indexing and retrieving programs like SUPERFILE, for example, assume that whatever text they analyze will be or has already been entered into microcomputer text files by your word processor; Nota Bene, a text management system designed specifically to meet the writing needs of academics and other researchers, provides word processor and full text data base indexing and retrieving functions in one package.[2]

General purpose *file* and *data base manager* programs are not created primarily to assist researchers in note-taking and file organizing. They are intended to assist business people in maintaining the information files that are crucial to their work. Nevertheless, their structure, data entry procedures, indexing, and retrieval capabilities may be easily adaptable to many such research tasks. For example, pfs:file, a popular file management program for Apple II and MS-DOS computers, allows you to define a "form" for the entry of almost any kind of information that can be divided into "fields" about almost any kind of unit that can be defined as a "record." Once the information has been entered, pfs:file will allow you to retrieve the information for any records by searching for key values or words.

Practically speaking, pfs:file works best, especially in its retrieval function, if the fields of its forms are filled with relatively brief entries. But there is no question that it would allow you to set up files of notes on a large variety of research topics. Figure 4.1 gives an example of a simple pfs:file form designed to support the entry of partially coded research notes about the occurrence and characteristics of coups d'etat.[3]

Once you had entered the information called for in the form of Figure 4.1 for the set of coups you were researching, you could easily recall any or all coups that had been characterized by "economic stagnation" as a justification, for example. If you needed it, you could ask the program to print out the form for each such coup. If you had a copy of pfs:file's companion report-generating program, pfs:report, you could have report prepare a formatted listing of all the instances of coups characterized by any particular set of traits. For ten coups, all this would hardly be necessary. For the hundreds that have occurred since the end of World War II, it would be a great boon.

Figure 4.2 gives an example of how a microcomputer data base manager program can be used for note-taking tasks. It illustrates the set up of a bibliography for dBASE II, the best known relational data base manager for CP/M and MS-DOS systems. The example is very simple and straightforward; you would most likely want to set up a number of other entries that specified a more concise author name or brief key words to speed up bibliographical searches.

Make no mistake: dBASE II was not created to be a bibliography manager. It is not meant to handle files of data with variable length fields like those in a bibliographical entry. Nevertheless, if you are willing to accept the wastage of disk space that will result from padding

---

COUNTRY: Abendia   COUP DATE: 01-16-82   SUCCESSFUL?: yes

COUP LEADER: Col. Corporativo Grieved DEGREE OF VIOLENCE: moderate

CONSOLIDATION DATE: 01-18-82   TERMINATION DATE: 06-23-84

TERMINATED BY: election

JUSTIFICATION KEYWORD 1: civilian corruption

JUSTIFICATION KEYWORD 2: street violence

JUSTIFICATION KEYWORD 3: economic stagnation

JUSTIFICATION KEYWORD 4: none

COMMENT: Parties banned/President Nerdowell jailed/President's private guard disbanded/legislature and courts left in session/ Col. Grieved promoted to Field Marshall 04-13-83

Figure 4.1:   A pfs: file Entry Form for Notes About Coups D'Etat

the end of its fixed length fields with blanks when entries do not take up all the field space allotted, it will make a fine one.

Once your bibliographical entries are in a dBASE II file, you will be able to use its standard commands to retrieve, sort, and list single items or groups of items by all or part of any field value. For example, if you wished to find a citation from among several hundred entries for which you have forgotten the author and exact title, but that you know had something to do with judges in Alberta, you could find it rather quickly be giving dBASE the appropriate command to search the title entry for the combination of the text strings "jud" and "Alberta."

The examples just given will demonstrate how standard business-oriented file and "relational" date base manager programs can be used to support a variety of note-taking and organizational tasks, even though they are not literally designed for such purposes. Researchers who have access to such microcomputer programs may find them very useful. On the other hand, it would not be wise to purchase such a program—particularly a relatively expensive one like dBASE II—to support these activities, unless you had other, probably more standard uses for it. If you want to invest in a program primarily for note-taking and organization, there are specialized programs that perform these tasks more directly, flexibly, and powerfully, usually at less cost. Two

```
AUTHOR :Falcon, Lawrence A. and Perry C. Smithson

TITLE  :Judicial  Authority  and the New  Canadian  Bill  of Rights -
Provincial Authority in the Alberta Native Peoples Case

                        :

JOURNAL :Alberta Law Review

VOLUME : 12:

NUMBER :1:

ISSUE :Spring                   :

YEAR :1983:

BEGINPAGE : 235:

ENDPAGE : 276:
```

Figure 4.2:   A dBASE II Bibliography Data Base Entry Form

programs that might serve as worthwhile examples of software specific-ally designed to support note-taking, indexing, and organization are CARDFILE and SUPERFILE.

Unlike the file and data base manager programs just discussed, both CARDFILE and SUPERFILE assume you will create the notes you wish to index and retrieve using your word processor. They do not require (or do not provide, depending on how you look at it) data entry into a form designed specifically for your particular current application.

CARDFILE is an example of an *index oriented* text retrieval system. As its name suggests, it seeks to emulate quite closely information storage, retrieval, and display in an index card file. It allows (requires) you to use the first 3 lines of a 21-line electronic "card" to record key word information identifying the card and its purposes, just as you might for a paper index card. It uses this information to find the cards you need quickly when you specify a search instruction. It can also search the remaining 18 lines of a card's text, if you so instruct it, to find information that you may not have recorded in the key word index lines. If you need a copy of any card(s), CARDFILE will print it for you.

Although not requiring the rigid formatting of information into fixed length fields like a file or data base manager, CARDFILE does impose some structure on the text of its electronic cards and reserves a fixed amount of disk space for each card. As a consequence, an individual card can have no more and no less than 18 (72 character) lines of text information in addition to its three lines of index information. You should be aware that this means that a CARDFILE file can hold approximately 100 cards on a double density single-sided diskette (like those for a Kaypro 2, for example). A little arithmetic will reveal that 21 lines of 72 characters each occupy 1572 bytes of storage. Even with no space required for program overhead (an unrealistic assumption), only 118 such cards could be stored on the 185k capacity Osborne 1 single-sided double density diskette on which the text for this section originally resided. On the other hand, the megabyte-sized floppy disk of an IBM-PC AT could contain over 800 such card records, and its 20-megabyte hard disk could in principle accommodate many thousands. Given the much greater capacity and speed of a 40-megabyte hard disk, or the gigabyte capacity of the optical disk you may have by 1988, you could have electronic index card files of a most imposing size indeed!

A second example of a program designed specifically to assist with the kinds of tasks involved in note-taking and organizing is SUPERFILE, a *text base system*. SUPERFILE is a "free format" indexing and information program. It will work on text files of any description and widely varying sizes created by any text editor.

SUPERFILE is able to have such flexibility because it indexes text files using key words or phrases specified for a file by its creator or user. The key words are entered directly into text files between special markers, and it is ordinarily possible to have the key words appear to the text formatter you use as non-printing "comments" so they do not affect printed versions of your text documents. The text files themselves do not have to reside on a single diskette. Indeed, if you create special text files consisting only of citations or location information and key words for text that is not in electronic form, the main text files do not have to reside in machine readable form at all. What must be available to SUPERFILE on a single diskette are the relatively compact index and dictionary files it uses in its work.

SUPERFILE'S approach means that it has great capacity. On a micro with 64K of memory it can use a key word dictionary of about 3000 words, and it always allows you to use the numbers from 0 to 31999 as key words without taking up any memory or disk space. The ability to use numbers as "free" key words can be very useful in retrieving dates, identification numbers, and so on. The number of indexed items of information it can handle at one time in one of its data bases is limited by disk size, but is over 1300 even for a vintage Xerox 820 single-sided single density diskette of 90K capacity, assuming each item has an average of 8 indexing key words and the indexing dictionary contains about 1200 words. Alternatively, on the double density Osborne 1 on which these words were written, it could accommodate nearly 3900 similarly indexed items with a maximum sized dictionary of over 2600 items. Its capacities are proportionately greater on a machine like the IBM-PC, or Texas Instruments Professional Computer on which this manuscript was revised. The 256K or larger memories and 360K floppy disk drives of such "PC class" computers greatly extend the limits of any data base or text indexing program, SUPERFILE included.

Remember that the size of the indexed text items is irrelevant to SUPERFILE. It will search the index for any data base of indexed items, retrieve the location of items matching the key words you have instructed it to look for, and instruct you to insert the particular diskette containing the item(s). It requires that you name diskettes containing data bases of items when the data bases are created so as you do not have to remember the location of the items when you want to find them again. Once the data base diskette is on line, SUPERFILE will display or print the appropriate items for your inspection.

Also remember that, unlike CARDFILE, SUPERFILE cannot search the text of the items it indexes, unless all the words in the text have been defined as keywords. Instead, it depends entirely upon your conscientious preparation of an appropriate list of key words for every item you want to have it index. Limitations of microcomputer speed and storage capacities make it impossible for the program to have both the capacity it does and an ability to search the huge volumes of text that capacity allows it to index. By forcing you to index with care the items you want to use in your research, SUPERFILE reinforces "good research habits" that some researchers may have abandoned. In return, it gives you control over masses of information that might simply be impossible to handle in a timely fashion using manual methods.

Realistically, researchers may have abandoned the kind of indexing SUPERFILE requires to work best because it is hard, non-creative work with no *immediate* payoff, precisely the kind of work a computer, not a human, should do. What these researchers need—and we count ourselves among them—is a text data base that will quickly and rapidly search the full text of research notes or documents for keywords defined ad hoc at the time the information is needed. Some mainframe information retrieval systems, the legal data base LEXIS, for example, will do this for a vast collection of court reports and other legal materials.

Microcomputer analogs of LEXIS and similar systems have not existed until recently. Even at this writing, it is not clear that a proven, affordable program that provides the ideal of full information retrieval wih no indexing in advance exists for any microcomputer likely to be owned by an individual researcher. A noteworthy example of a program that makes a good effort to provide researchers the integrated word processing and text base functions they need is Nota Bene but it still requires serious attention to indexing prior to the creation of a text data base. An example of a data base manager that provides a great deal of the flexibility in file organization and indexing needed by researchers at an affordable price is the Nutshell Information Manager. Both programs are for IBM-PCs and PC-compatible computers.

Word Processing for
Questionnaire Construction

Constructing the questionnaires researchers use to gather survey data is an iterative task. Question texts must be carefully examined and pretested for clarity, reliability, and validity. Interviewer instructions must similarly be carefully reviewed for intelligibility and lack of bias. The format of the questionnaire instrument must be designed to promote maximum accuracy and efficiency in recording responses. Alternative versions of the instrument may need to be prepared for administration to selected subsamples. All these requirements mean that the text of a typical questionnaire can benefit enormously from processing on a microcomputer.

Automated Survey Research

One of the areas in which exciting advances are being made with the application of microcomputers is in survey research. The development of Computer-Aided Telephone Interviewing (CATI) systems at the

Survey Research Center, University of Michigan, and elsewhere on minicomputer and mainframe systems, has stimulated the production of similar systems using microcomputers. Merrill Shanks and his colleagues in the Computer-Assisted Survey Methods Program at the University of California, Berkeley; Charles Pallit at the Survey Research Laboratory, University of Wisconsin, Madison; and Bruce Brock at the School of Public Health, University of Michigan are all working on systems that use microcomputers to aid in the survey data collection process.

Each of these systems is somewhat different, both in design and function, but they share some common features. Interviewers are seated at microcomputers, and administer a survey instrument that appears on the screen. As respondents answer the survey questions, the interviewers enter their responses on the micro. The microcomputer can then check the responses to ensure that valid codes are being entered by the interviewer, and that the responses are logically consistent with previous answers. The micro can also control the order in which the questions are asked, and skip questions or otherwise move around the survey instrument as called for by the survey design, without intervention from the interviewer. These systems can also be set up so that respondents can sit at the microcomputer and themselves enter the answers to survey questions. After the data have been collected, the micros can then be used to generate reports of the survey results.

In addition, some of these systems have elaborate methods to help provide process control for the survey researcher. They may generate the phone numbers for telephone interviewers to dial, keep lists of names and other information on sampling units, keep track of follow-up interviews, and provide audit trails for tracking down problems. Some provide systems that help in coding "open ended" question responses, and allow researchers on different work stations to send electronic mail or participate in conferences.

These kinds of features enable researchers to use survey instruments that are much larger and more complex than those ordinarily administered by human interviewers alone. They also provide a much greater degree of control over the survey process than has previously been available. These kinds of systems are leading the way in the application of microcomputers in data collection and process control.

Data Gathering in the Field

Microcomputers, especially those in portable or transportable packages, provide viable and cost-effective alternatives to pencils and paper as tools for collecting data in the field. We conceive the distinction between portable and transportable computers a little differently from the manufacturers. To our way of thinking, a portable microcomputer is one that operates on batteries but has substantial and significant computing power—not just an expanded calculator. Transportable systems, by way of contrast, are those packaged to be easily carried about, but not necessarily capable of being operated independently of standard electrical sources. The portable systems of the mid-80s include machines such as the Tandy (Radio Shack) Executive 100 and more powerful systems like the Hewlett-Packard 110, the Data General/One, and the Texas Instruments Pro-Lite. There are transportable versions of the IBM PC and other 16-bit machines that are designed to be packed up in a single unit with handles. The Apple Macintosh and 8-bit computers such as the Kaypro and Osborne are also transportable.

The portable movement was spurred by the introduction of the Osborne 1 in the early 1980s although the Osborne was the first of the transportable, not portable, systems. Although the portable computers typically weigh under ten pounds, the transportable systems range from about 25 pounds to over 40 pounds and are usually of a size that can be carried under the seat of an airplane. The portable systems, with selected peripheral devices, are often about the size of a large-city telephone book. Memory sizes range from about 32K to 256K or more and have a variety of both specialized peripherals, such as bar code readers, and general peripherals, such as tape or disk drives are available.

Potentially there are a large number of applications for data-gathering in the field with portable and transportable machines. In the social and behavioral sciences a common problem is capturing the results of face-to-face or telephone interviews. It would be a relatively trivial programming problem to create either a specialized or general program to capture interview data. In fact, such a program could be structured so that the computer was simply set up for the respondent to enter the data directly on the keyboard, or, alternatively, have the interviewer record the data directly as with a CATI system. Some hospitals and physicians are already using such systems to take medical histories—a similar data collection problem.

Although the initial cost of purchase of transportable or portable systems for the application suggested can be relatively large, substantial savings in time and money can be achieved because the data are already in machine-readable form and need not be converted by human data-entry operators (or perhaps by optical mark-reading equipment). The human engineering problems involved in having respondents directly enter data on a keyboard are considerably less than having them fill in a questionnaire or worse, an optical mark answer sheet. The memories of the portable and transportable systems now available are sufficiently large to allow the acquisition of data from several respondents and those data can then be stored for further use on tape, diskettes, or sent across telephone lines to another target computer for analysis.

Process Control in
Experimental Research

Related to the issues raised in the preceding section is the extension of automated research procedures through *process control*. Process control can be defined as the use of computers and programs to control complex processes. The term has been applied most extensively in industries where computers control machines in manufacturing processes, but it is also applicable in the automated control of experimental research. The concept of process control is better established in some of the physical sciences, such as physics or chemistry, than it is in the social and behavioral sciences. It is true, nevertheless, that for the purpose of controlling experiments and collecting information from those experiments, behavioral scientists could also benefit substantially. In such situations researchers might well use portable or transportable systems, but could just as well use desk-top units.

A number of years ago one of us published an early effort (Madron, 1969) suggesting that experimental designs were relevant to the study of politics, especially the politics of small groups. The various research techniques it described were technologically primitive in comparison to what can be accomplished in the 1980s. Yet even in 1969, it tried to suggest ways in which data collection in small group situations might have been automated. Today, contemporary microcomputers can often handle "real-time" timing control, data recording, and the related problems of process control better than can large, central, multi-user systems.

With small group research in the several disciplines doing such work, microcomputers can, today, be set up as part of the structure of small group experiments. Some small group interaction techniques, for example, require participants to respond in various ways (or at least record the way in which participants respond) to interaction stimuli as group discussions occur. If each participant is provided a device much like a "joy stick" used with computer games, that person can then dynamically record responses to the group processes taking place. If, in addition, simple sensors are added that record such physiological responses as galvanic skin resistance, heartbeat, and other factors, then these can also be recorded as the experiment proceeeds. It should also be noted that similar technology can be employed in planning a forecasting environment creating a situation for on-line, dynamic systems using modifications of the Delphi Method developed by the Rand Corporation in the 1960s. Although the initial investment in such lab equipment might seem high, these kinds of devices are easily employed for a wide variety of projects and are not as expensive as many other peripheral devices.

Communications for Data Transferral

Certainly, when a contemporary research facility is designed, care should be taken to ensure that laboratories can be completely wired to provide the networking required for support of the techniques implied previously. Such data communications networks, sometimes referred to as "local area networks," may include only microcomputers and their peripherals, or may also include nodes linking mainframe computers into the system. Some contemporary networks allow the concurrent communications of data, video, and voice. The concurrent use of all three facilities is highly desirable in a number of laboratory and experimental situations in both the physical and behavioral sciences. Certainly that would be highly desirable in small group research. Very frequently the only communications facility needed, however, is the ability to "upload" data from a micro to a larger computer, or to "download" data in the opposite direction. There are several issues of which you should be aware.

HARDWARE

The hardware is referred to as a *communications interface,* and there are several varieties. The most common hardware interface is designed to provide an RS-232-C, serial asynchronous communications capability. Asynchronous communications (sometimes called "start/stop") transmit and receive a single eight-bit character at a time. The two ends of the connection know when to transmit and when to receive by a start and stop bit that precedes and succeeds each byte of data. The RS-232-C standard is an assignment of specific communications functions to each of 25 wires in a special multiwire cable. Computers and other devices using this standard thus are using the same wires for the same functions, and can communicate with each other.

Alternatives or additions might be a communications board that would allow synchronous communications. Synchronous devices transmit and receive blocks of data synchronized by timing signals. A *modem,* or modulator-demodulator, is also often needed for data communications. A modem allows the digital signals generated by the computer to be transmitted over telephone or other communications lines, and is necessary to send and receive data on dial-up systems and some types of local area networks. The typical configuration for the older, smaller systems, such as the Apple II or TRS-80 series, was to install an asynchronous serial communications board in the machine, which attached to an external modem. With the newer 16-bit systems such as the IBM PC, a far larger number of options are available.

With the newer, larger machines it is possible to get a combined interface board that includes both a serial interface circuit and a built-in modem that attaches directly to a telephone line. If you will be using the system exclusively with telephone communications this can be an excellent option. Some of the boards also support synchronous as well as asynchronous communications. Examples of these boards are those produced by Texas Instruments for the TI Professional Computer: a synch/asynch card and an internal modem card, both of which can handle either synchronous or asynchronous communications. Most private use of communications will require only asynchronous systems, but this is not invariably the case. There are, in addition, systems becoming available allowing for voice communications between or among microcomputers such as the Texas Instruments Speech Command System and the Tecmar Voice Recognition and Speech Command add-on boards for IBM and other 8088 computers.

SOFTWARE

When selecting microcomputer software for research, it is extremely important to take communications needs into account. If the communications problem is primarily concerned with data collection and analysis, one set of problems occur. Most communications programs available for micros are capable of reasonably fast and reliable transmission of data from one microcomputer to another. Not all communications programs are suitable for transferring data from and to mainframe computers, however—particularly mainframes running IBM operating systems.

This problem may have arisen because communications software developers have until recently perceived the home market as their primary target, and many of these developers seem to have had little experience with large mainframes. But most researchers require communications with IBM-style systems, and many also require communications with other vendors' computers. It is therefore critical that the capacity for communications, especially data transferral, with appropriate mainframes be ascertained before communications software is purchased. You should consult with your central computing facility to find out what communications software is supported. Some university computing centers will be able to provide you with communications programs free or at a reduced charge. One such program, KERMIT, was developed at Columbia University to meet exactly the kinds of problems researchers face.

If it is necessary to access remote systems such as DIALOG for bibliographic searches, then other problems occur. In fact, some newer software is now becoming available for the 8088 class machines that make it much easier for a user to access services like DIALOG. That software will allow, largely through a menu-driven system, the researcher to set up a DIALOG search off-line on the micro, then automatically attach to DIALOG, submit the search, and return, thus saving communications and search costs. The moral of all this is that it is likely that you will need more than one communications program to do all the communications necessary in a modern scientific environment.

ASYNCHRONOUS SYSTEMS

The choice here is very wide with an extremely wide variation in type and quality of programs. The simplest asynchronous communications program is sometimes referred to as a "dumb" terminal program. Such a program simply gives you access to the mainframe asynchronous communications hardware and acts like a simple teletype machine—it will not have the capacity to transfer files, address the screen, or provide other services that might be necessary. On the other hand, if all you have to do is communicate with a large mainframe system as a dumb terminal, then this kind of program is for you. It has the further advantage of being very cheap.

The better, more intelligent programs provide a wide variety of services in addition to simple communications. They often provide file transfer capabilities—a very important function—full control of the hardware, the ability to access the operating system of the micro and its software, and other features. Examples of such programs are ASCOM, Ascii Express, CrossTalk, TELETERM, VTERM, and Z-Term Pro, among others. These are available for a wide variety of CPUs, including 6502, Z80 (8080), and 8088 systems.

Good communications programs also "emulate" one or more standard terminals, such as DEC's VT100 or Lear-Siegler's ADM3A terminals. The advantage of having terminal emulation capabilities is that there is a large variety of software and hardware available that requires that emulation. For example, at our institution, North Texas State University, we have standardized on a VT100 compatible terminal and terminal emulator. This is because we have both IBM-compatible mainframes as well as DEC's VAX 11/780 super minicomputers. With a VT100 type terminal we can access the IBM-compatible systems through a protocol converter that makes a VT100, among other terminals, look like an IBM 3270 type terminal. This means that users can have full-screen editing and other capabilities on either the IBM-type systems or on the VAXs *from the same terminal.*

SYNCHRONOUS SYSTEMS IN AN
IBM MAINFRAME ENVIRONMENT

In particular institutional environments it may be possible to use IBM-specific communications: 3270 transactional terminal systems or 3780 remote job entry (RJE) terminals. Synchronous communications is further complicated by the fact that IBM currently uses two different synchronous protocols: bisynchronous (bsc or bisynch) and SDLC/SNA. The two are not compatible with one another. With 3270 type communications the 3270 terminal must be plugged into a "cluster controller," which supports a number of terminals (up to 32).

The 3780 RJE software is designed primarily for file transfer from one system to another. A 3780 is primarily designed to run batches of data (a deck of cards, for example, or their logical equivalent) to and from another system. The 3780 protocol provides very solid communications. Although the 3780 is an IBM protocol, it has also been implemented on a number of other systems including DEC's VAX series and Hewlett-Packard's 3000 series. Two micros running 3780 software can also communicate with one another. If your problem is primarily that of transferring large quantities of data from one system to another in a reliable fashion, then this alternative may prove to be very attractive.

On the whole, data transfer is somewhat faster using synchronous protocols than asynchronous systems, even when running at the same line speed. This happens because data are sent in multibyte blocks with the synchronous systems, rather than in single bytes, thus reducing overhead in data transmissions. In most circumstances, however, it is necessary to work *very* closely with your central computer center to use synchronous communications effectively.

SPECIALIZED COMMUNICATIONS OPTIONS

There is a considerable amount of specialized communications software and hardware now coming on the market for use with microcomputers. One class of software can best be described as "front ends" for specialized remote services such as Dow Jones or DIALOG. With these products it is possible to save communications costs by setting up and debugging searches for information locally, then having the micro call the particular service and do the search. The further advantage of such front ends is that the time required to learn to do an effective search, especially in a complicated database like DIALOG, is considerably reduced.

We have briefly mentioned a class of networks called *local area networks* or LANs. For a large research project with a number of microcomputer-based work stations it might prove to be useful to link those micros together in a LAN. A LAN typically provides some services such as file or print servers, which allow some economy of scale for expensive peripherals. In addition, it is also possible to run electronic mail systems across a LAN, thus improving communications among those involved in the research project. If the LAN is not to be connected into a larger, campus-wide, communications system, then there are a number of technologies that might be used. The system that has received the most publicity is Ethernet, a system developed by Xerox, with products now being made by a number of manufacturers. Ethernet products are typically available only for the 16-bit systems, however.

Local area networks come in many different configurations or "topologies." In Figure 4.3 we have depicted a number of different networking configurations. Large scale networks are typically configured as point-to-point, multipoint, star, or hierarchical systems. LANs usually use a bus, ring, or star topology. The most common LAN topology, exemplified by IBM's PC Network or Xerox's Ethernet, is the bus. Very high speed systems often use a ring structure, and networks based on telephony use stars.

There are many LANs that are designed only for micros. There are others that are engineered for both micros and mainframe environments. If you have a mixture of devices—new 16-bit micros, older 8-bit machines, and miscellaneous other equipment as well as access to mainframe or minicomputer ports—then a LAN that uses an RS-232-C serial communications interface will provide the most universal connectivity. Such systems can be acquired from manufacturers like Sytek, Inc., 3M, or Ungermann-Bass. LANs are classified as either baseband or broadband. A baseband system can run on either coaxial cable or twisted pairs of copper wire and a device places an unmodulated signal on the cable. A broadband system typically uses cable television technology and produces a modulated radio frequency signal that runs over a

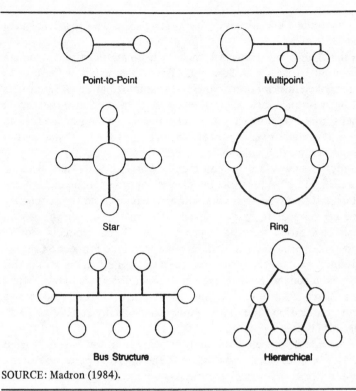

Point-to-Point

Multipoint

Star

Ring

Bus Structure

Hierarchical

SOURCE: Madron (1984).

Figure 4.3: Characteristic Network Configurations

coaxial cable. IBM's PC Network is a broadband system; Xerox's Ethernet is a baseband system.

With a large-scale research project it may be desirable for the participants in the project to be able to share and update files in order to improve productivity or to implement other subsystems, such as automated survey research. If project members are working out in the field, or at other than standard hours, then an electronic mail system can improve and facilitate communications among the members of the team. Manuscripts being developed by several different members of the project could be easily transferred back and forth at will. All of these functions could be made available through the use of a local area network.

On the slightly more esoteric end of the communications issue are microcomputer-based voice systems. These systems allow the user to capture spoken information and record that information as digital files on a floppy or hard disk, then transmit them to or receive them from another similarly equipped system. The micro receiving such a file can then play them back over a speaker. Through the use of such devices it is possible to establish a voice-based electronic mail system.

Finally, a new class of communications software has become available in mid-1984 for those people with appropriate access to large mainframe systems: software that allows the micro user to use the disk storage capacity of the mainframe as a virtual desk peripheral. An example is a product called Micro-Tempus. Such products require software at both the micro and mainframe end of the connection. At the micro end, the software overlays the operating system (MS-DOS in this instance) and adds what appears to be another disk drive to the system. When a file is written or read to that "virtual" disk, however, the data go up a communications line to the mainframe—usually an IBM or IBM-compatible computer.

On the mainframe end, the data are captured and saved in what appears to be a format compatible with the micro's operating system. Some additional mainframe utilities may be available that allow the transfer of information from the mainframe's database system to the micro's virtual disk, or vice versa. The advantage of this arrangement is that the mainframe system will have very large amounts of disk space, but, even more important, will have standard procedures to backup and protect the data—a constant problem for microcomputer users. Such a product cannot be casually acquired and demands the active cooperation of the central computing facility.

For Further Reading

Reviews of general file and data base managers for 8088 class machines are contained in Heintz (1983a and 1984) and Abbott (1983). There are also books dedicated to particular data base packages. See Date (1983) and Heiser (1984) for examples.

There are a number of good books on microcomputer communications commonly available that you might consult: Derfler and Stallings (1983), Glossbrenner (1983), Jordan and Churchill (1983), Madron (1984), Nichols et al. (1982), and Nilles (1983).

5. DATA ANALYSIS AND MANIPULATION

Data analysis is the task that social and behavioral scientists most frequently associate with the computer. The previous sections of this book have attempted to show that computers, and especially microcomputers, are reasonable and useful tools for a wide variety of other tasks connected with the research process. It is true, however, that computers are designed to analyze data, especially the numerically coded data we often collect in the course of research. In this section of the monograph we will discuss how microcomputers are suited (and sometimes not suited) to this task, and to other types of analysis that are not quite so frequently carried out with the aid of computers.

Statistical Analysis
on Microcomputers

The advantages and disadvantages of conducting statistical analyses on micros are determined by the quality of the two factors that affect the usefulness of any computer: hardware and software. Microcomputer hardware is still, as of this writing, fairly constrained in terms of the speed of the CPUs and I/O paths, the amount of memory the CPUs can address, and the quantity of data that can be stored on disk. The boundaries of these constraints are being rapidly enlarged as manufacturers race to increase the size and speed of their machines, but it may be a few years before significant advances are widely available at low cost. Statistical software, partly because of the limitations imposed by hardware, and partly because of inexperience or unfamiliarity with the needs of serious researchers on the part of software developers, is often inadequate or hard to use. At the same time, the size and sophistication of the kinds of problems social and behavioral scientists are addressing are increasing. These factors lead us to the conclusion that micro-computers cannot, at present, fulfill the data analysis needs of every researcher. It is still true, however, that microcomputers alone can do the job well for many researchers and a wide variety of research problems, and in combination with communications software and access to large mainframes, can make any data analysis quicker and easier.

Statistical software for microcomputers can be categorized into two broad classes: software originally written for mainframe or other large computers and adapted to micros, and software written originally for microcomputers. In the first category we find, or will soon find, the statistical packages with which you are already familiar from the mainframe world: SPSS^x, BMDP, Minitab, and SAS. In the second category there are dozens of packages available, including general purpose packages modeled on the mainframe systems, and packages that are limited to only a few statistical applications.

Statistical packages that were originally written for mainframe computers, and have been adapted to run on microcomputers, may offer you some real advantages. First, you may already know how to use the software, and will not have to invest a significant amount of time learning how to use the program. Second, many of these programs contain powerful facilities to transform, recode, or otherwise manipulate your data. Third, mainframe packages often provide a wide variety of useful statistical procedures. Finally, the algorithms used in the calculations have been tested by thousands of users under many different conditions. Although adapting a mainframe program to run on a microcomputer may require some rewriting, experienced statistical programmers may transport the algorithms with few, if any, modifications. You may have some confidence in their results.

There is, of course, another side to the coin. These statistical packages will require much larger microcomputers in order to work. Thus, your investment in hardware may be significantly higher. In addition, not every procedure in the mainframe version of the package may be available on the micro. Some statistical procedures require programs that are too big for the resources of any computer currently classified as a micro. Finally, the cost of these programs will be substantially higher than some packages that have been written especially for microcomputers. As a micro user, you are not participating in the economies of scale that can be applied in the mainframe environment. Buying a fully-blown statistical package may mean that you spend a lot of money on statistical procedures that you will rarely or never use. On the other hand, universities and other organizations will probably work out arrangements with software suppliers that will make these products available at reduced prices. You should consider these benefits and costs carefully when purchasing a statistical package for your micro.

The statistical packages that have been written especially for microcomputers are numerous and varied. They include a range of programs, from those capable of only rudimentary descriptive statistics, to those that contain the most commonly used procedures, those that are fully-blown competitors to mainframe packages. There are also a few special-purpose packages for methods such as exploratory data analysis and Box-Jenkins analysis.

Like the mainframe statistical packages discussed above, these programs have their good and bad points. Many have only limited recoding and variable transformation capabilities, and they can be pretty picky about the kinds of data they will accept. Some, for instance, can't handle blank data fields or special missing value codes. Most do not contain the more advanced statistical procedures, such as multivariate analysis of variance. A more serious potential problem is that the algorithms used by these packages are sometimes untested. This can cause results to be affected by accumulated rounding errors and other mathematical quirks. Some packages, however, have quite elaborate data entry facilities, and almost all of them run on micros with fairly standard configurations. There are a few that are reasonably inexpensive, even cheap. Before purchasing any statistical package, you should investigate it carefully through reviews in the microcomputer press, inquiries directed to those who have used the program, and, if possible, test the program by running the statistical procedures you intend to use on data and hardware similar to those on which you intend to use them.

Of more than a dozen statistical packages we reviewed in preparing this monograph, few provided more than rudimentary graphics capabilities (Statpro is one exception). There are graphics packages that can read data output from a statistical package, however, and the popularity of software such as Lotus 1-2-3, which combines graphics with other analytical applications, ensures that statistical programs for micros will soon implement graphics features. Many microcomputers make fine graphics display devices, and low-cost plotters and graphics printers are available.

It is clear from the preceding discussion that there is a wide variety of statistical software available for microcomputers. There are also many other data analytic tools that you may find useful for research. These include not only data base management systems, but also word processing and spreadsheet software.

Data Base, Spreadsheet, and Word Processor
Programs as Data Managers/Manipulators

As you have seen, one of the major differences between statistical analysis on a microcomputer and statistical analysis using a mature mainframe statistical package like BMDP, SAS, or SPSS^x, and also one of the biggest weaknesses of microcomputer software designed for statistical analysis, is the limited ability of the micro software to perform the powerful data management actions, manipulations, and transformations that are routinely available in the mainframe software. Certainly progress in microcomputer statistical software is being made, and some currently available—if expensive—statistical packages have substantial data manipulation capabilities. Nevertheless, for the near future many microcomputer users who need to do statistical analysis on their machines will find their needs are not met by the statistical software available to them.

Fortunately, if you want to use a micro to do statistical analysis and find that your statistical software does not meet your data management needs, you may possess other software that provides substantial data manipulation capabilities. The capabilities of a data base manager can allow you to create a new, thoroughly transformed data set for analysis by your statistical programs. For sufficiently small data sets, so may an electronic spreadsheet. Even your text editor may provide some data transformation capacity and ease the task of directly changing small amounts of data so that you can get your data in shape for statistical analysis.

Let's take up the last point first. Text editors are not designed to function as manipulators of data. Indeed, because they do not ordinarily even recognize numeric data as numeric, one certainly could not perform arithmetic transformations with a word processor's text editor.

Nevertheless, much data manipulation involves "recoding," substituting one value for another. Given the abilty to identify clearly particular data values that need to be transformed to other values, a word processor's global search and replace capability can provide a direct way to make recoding changes reasonably quickly and reliably. Because most global search and replace capabilities allow you to mandate that your consent be given before any change is made, you can, for a small cost in time, use the search and replace function with confidence that only proper changes will be made.

In like manner, the ability of most text editors to merge other files at any appropriate place into the text file currently being edited gives them the equivalent of an "add cases" function like that of SPSS^x and other mainframe data analysis packages. If your text editor has a "column move" capabilitity, it will make it possible for you to "add variables" to the records of an existing file. To do this, you would first read into the existing data file (at its end) a second file containing the new data needed to add the variables to the existing file. You would then mark the new data as a column to be moved, and finally moved it to the column adjacent to the last data column of the first row of the existing data set. (This is easier to do than it is to describe!) Wordstar, among other packages, has this capability, but it is not available with every word processor.

If the changes you need to make to the records of an existing data set cannot be accomplished through either of the methods just described, you will at least find that your text editor's text manipulation capability makes it relatively easy to go through your file to make necessary changes on a record by record basis.

Standard spreadsheet programs like VisiCalc, Supercalc, Multiplan, or Lotus 1-2-3 can provide very substantial data transformation and manipulation capabilities, provided the Ns of your data sets do not exceed the spreadsheet's row limits or the total quantity of data and formulas required do not cause you to exceed available memory. Spreadsheets can do most if not all the numeric transformations that mainframe statistical packages can perform, including conditional changes or transformations based on "if" statements and, through the use of "lookup tables," most recoding tasks as well. Once the necessary data manipulations have been completed, you may be able to have the spreadsheet save the new data set to disk in a format that your statistical package can use. Failing that, you can certainly have the data "printed," possibly without borders or complicating labels, to disk instead of paper. If necessary, you can then edit the standard text file thus created with your text editor to remove unnecessary text or quickly add needed text (perhaps separating commas) to make the data set ready for statistical analysis.

Data transformation with a microcomputer data base manager is very similar to data transformation and manipulation with a mainframe data analysis package, as long as the data set is not too large for convenient manipulation with the microcomputer program. Even when the whole data base is too large—as, for example, when you need to use more than the 32 variables a data base manager like dBASE II allows— you may be able to break it up into manageable pieces than can be manipulated with a micro data base manager and reassembled (perhaps with a sort/merge program or even a "column-moving" text editor) for statistical analysis.

Once you have used dBASE II (or another data base manager) to create a new data file incorporating the recoding and data trans- formations necessary for your statistical analysis, you will need to have the data base manager write out a version of the file that can be read by your statistical program. Good data base managers can routinely provide you with fixed variables in fixed length records, records with commas delimiting variables, or, at least in the case of dBASE II, other possibilities. As a worst case, you can have the data base manager "print" the data records to a disk file that you can edit with your text editor to remove unnecessary material prior to submitting the data file to your statistical program.

Using Spreadsheet Programs
for Data Analysis

Programs such as VisiCalc, Lotus 1-2-3, or Multiplan, although not designed to perform statistical analysis, often contain some statistical functions, and can be adapted easily to produce other statistics. This can be especially important if you do not have a large amount of data to process, if you do not require advanced multivariate analysis, or if your budget will not allow access to more sophisticated statistical software on your micro or mainframe computer.

As we mentioned earlier, a spreadsheet program organizes numbers into rows and columns, and then allows you to perform operations on the rows and columns, or on cells formed by the row and column intersections. This row-and-column organization is similar in spirit to the way statistical software organizes data for analysis, with rows representing cases or observations, and columns representing variables. In addition, most spreadsheet programs provide in their catalog of operations some simple statistical functions and the ability to define rows, columns, or cells in terms of formulas. Therefore, if you enter data for analysis into a spreadsheet program, each case in its own row and each variable in its own column, you can "teach" your spreadsheet program to do statistics. As an example, let's teach Multiplan to calculate a Pearson's product-moment correlation (r).

The correlation of two variables X and Y is defined as the covariance of X and Y divided by the product of their standard deviations. Multiplan has a standard deviation function, called STDEV, so we can obtain the standard deviations quite easily. We enter the data for X and Y in two columns, use the NAME function provided by Multiplan to refer to the columns (simply naming them "X" and "Y"), and define a couple of cells somewhere convenient on the spreadsheet as STDEV(X) and STDEV(Y). As soon as we define these cells, Multiplan calculates these statistics and places the values in the cells. Now, let's NAME these two cells "SDX" and "SDY," so that we can use them later.

Getting the covariance is a slightly more complicated process. A useful computational formula for the covariance of X and Y is:

$$\sum_{i=1}^{N} \frac{X_i Y_i - N\overline{X}\overline{Y}}{N-1}$$

which requires us to come up with four values: the sum over all the cases of the product of X and Y; the number of cases; the mean of X; and the mean of Y. Three of these values are easy to get, as Multiplan has a function to calculate the mean, called AVERAGE, and to get the number of cases, called COUNT. We must merely define three cells as AVERAGE (X), AVERAGE (Y), and COUNT(X), and then NAME them "MEANX," "MEANY," and "N." To get the sum of products, we define a cell in a column adjacent to the X and Y columns, using Multiplan's multiplication operator "*," as X*Y. We must then copy

X	47	Y	33	XY	1551	MEANX	MEANY	SUMXY
	54		49		2646	48.571429	39.035714	53554
	48		40		1920			
	47		44		2068	N	SDX	SDY
	50		48		2400	28	4.2463803	6.0398807
	45		36		1620			
	50		35		1750	COVXY	PEARSON'S R	
	56		50		2800	17.238095	0.6721126	
	54		46		2484			
	48		37		1776			
	53		40		2120			
	47		39		1833			
	38		32		1216			
	47		42		1974			
	48		39		1872			
	49		37		1813			
	53		42		2226			
	53		40		2120			
	49		40		1960			
	52		47		2444			
	40		37		1480			
	48		34		1632			
	43		21		903			
	50		40		2000			
	49		34		1666			
	52		39		2028			
	48		38		1824			
	42		34		1428			

Figure 5.1: A Multiplan Spreadsheet for Calculating Pearson's r

this formula to the other cells in the column using the COPY command. We name this column "XY," and then define a cell as SUM(XY), using the SUM function to get the total. Once again, we'll NAME this cell, calling it "SUMXY." Now that we have all the pieces for the covariance formula, we can define another cell as (SUMXY-N*MEANX* MEANY)/(N-1), which gives us the covariance. If we NAME this cell "COVXY," we can get the correlation coefficient by defining a last cell as COVXY/(SDX*SDY). Figure 5.1 shows, with the addition of cell and column labels, the results of this procedure for some scores on first and second midterm examinations for 28 introductory statistics students (Hopkins and Glass, 1978: 125).

This type of procedure can be easily extended to other statistics, such as regression coefficients, analysis of variance, and measures of association for cross-classifications. Some advantages of organizing a spreadsheet in this way include its ability to serve as a "template," as the layout of the spreadsheet and its formulas can be saved to disk and recalled for use later. The data for any two variables can be entered in the X and Y columns, and the program will apply the formulas you have stored. The key to versatility here is to keep the format and the assigned names and formulas as generalized as possible, so that the template is flexible enough to handle a variety of data.

Spreadsheet programs do, clearly, have limitations as tools for data analysis. Most programs have strict constraints on the number of rows and columns they can contain. Multiplan, for instance, can use only 255 rows and 63 columns. If your data contained more than 255 cases, you would have to put the program through further contortions to calculate your statistics. Spreadsheet programs cannot as yet perform linear algebraic operations, such as taking the inverse of a matrix, and most are not truly programmable. It would therefore be an extremely complex process to train them to do multiple regression with a number of independent variables, or to do factor analysis. These inabilities also rule out the application of many of the advanced algorithms, such as those based on sweep operations, that are used by sophisticated statistical programs for speed and accuracy. In spite of these problems, however, spreadsheet programs can do some kinds of statistical analysis fairly readily. When this is coupled with the fact that oftentimes spreadsheet programs are included "free" with the purchase of a microcomputer, their attractiveness as data analytic tools is considerably enhanced.

Using Computers for Textual Analysis

During the early sixties, when computing was relatively in its infancy, considerable work was done pointing toward automated techniques of content analysis. Content analysis is a quantitative extension of traditional analytical research in that the effort is made to code text and assign numerical values to portions of the text for later statistical analysis. An example of such early efforts was *The General Inquirer* (Stone, 1966). Largely due to a lack of funding those early efforts at automating content analysis stopped sometime in the late sixties or early seventies. With major improvements in computer technology, the time is ripe for a renewed effort in this area.

A somewhat related use of computers in the analysis of documents is their use in authenticity studies. One of the classic examples was the assignment of authorship of each of *The Federalist Papers* by Mosteller and Wallace (1964). More recently, similar techniques have been applied to the Bible by biblical scholars. If authenticity is not a problem, then the editing of editions of the works of major historical figures can be simplified and quickened through the use of computers.

Finally, in many disciplines today computers are routinely used to assist in the bibliographic work that is a necessary prelude to any serious research. Services such as DIALOG, owned by Lockheed (California), are accessible through virtually all research libraries in the United States. Although DIALOG is geared for the physical sciences, social sciences, and business, similar systems would be possible and appropriate for more specialized study areas. The advantage of doing bibliographic searches by computer is that if the bibliographic database has been established, such a search is inevitably more complete than one done by hand sitting in a library. Related computer applications include information retrieval of newspaper based information from such "information utilities" as the Source or Compuserve. Through these sources one can look at current newspapers, the UPI wire service, or segments of the *New York Times* archive.

SOFTWARE, HARDWARE, AND INFORMATIONAL NEEDS

Clearly, computers can be used in the analysis, editing, and manipulation of textual materials as well as for numerical and statistical analysis. But can it be done easily? It can be done with at least moderate ease, and some of the appropriate software is available, either for microcomputers or for large mainframe computers. To make the process of computer assisted analysis of historical materials more easily available to a wide community of scholars; however, some additional development would be helpful. In particular, there should be some additional software development, and there must be some collective effort to translate bodies of materials into machine-readable form.

Software needs. Although there is an ever increasing amount of software (computer programs) available for the manipulation of text, much of the current development comes from the needs for increasing levels of office automation. Many of the word processing systems currently on the market can be used "off the shelf" to assist with the manipulation of text. The development of both software and data resources can be traced to a large extent in the pages of a journal called *Computers and the Humanities.* Increasingly, however, more popular computer oriented magazines are featuring articles that should be of interest to traditional scholars.

Specialized text editors that would assist in the generation of notes (not just computerized note-taking programs), in the sorting of notes, and in the decomposition of text for content analysis would be useful. That development is unlikely to come about, however, until scholars develop greater acceptance of computers as an aid to textual research. Conversely, such software development is not likely to take place without the active endorsement of groups concerned with specific areas of interest. The fact must be faced that much software development, even in universities, is a function of demand (or the market, if you will). Software will not be developed if there is not a perceived market for the product.

Hardware and data resources. Even though some additional software development would be desirable, the fact is that there is a considerable amount of "off the shelf" software already in existence. What is not available in many areas of study, especially those needing textual information, is a corpus of machine-readable documents. If text is entered by traditional data entry techniques with people keying in the text, the cost works out to $2 to $3 (U.S.) per page, assuming about 500 words per printed page. There are automated techniques for translating text to machine-readable form, however. One machine, manufactured by Kurzweil, Inc. (recently acquired by Xerox), can read most English type fonts, and time can be purchased for about $1.25/1000 characters. From the perspective of microcomputer users, however, even more exciting developments are taking place. At a computer trade show in May 1984 (COMDEX), a low-cost character reader for micros was announced (for a list price of $495) that would read several standard character fonts, and, in addition, had a learning mode that enabled it to read—and enter—textual data from a very wide variety of printed fonts.

Another source of machine-readable text should be publishers, many of whom already use computerized typesetting or composition techniques. At some point just after the middle of this decade it will be possible to use video laser disks as the medium of storage, and an author's entire corpus could be placed on a single disk. In the meantime, a standard "floppy disk" format might be appropriate.

Similarly, a machine-readable bibliographic database would be very helpful to scholars in specialized fields. The appropriate approach might well be a system based on microcomputers using "off the shelf" data management software for retrieval. Within the context of a network of scholars, if a standardized format for bibliographic resources were adopted, it would be possible to generate a significant amount of data at a relatively low cost. Some organizing agency would still be required, however.

Suffice it to say that computers lie in the future of even the most tradition-bound disciplines. It does not make a great deal of sense to continue to do time-consuming tasks with any but the best tools. Computers from the smallest to the largest provide a new set of information processing tools as did the technologies of writing and printing in other eras. To use computers effectively it is not necessary, or even necessarily desirable, for everyone to become a computer expert. To use a typewriter effectively, after all, it not necessary to know how to build one. On the other hand, tools like computers cannot be used well if we restrict our imaginations and refuse to recognize the role computers can play regardless of our discipline. We have before us today the relatively cheap availability of one of the more powerful tools yet developed—we should try to use it effectively.

Communications for Large-Scale Analysis

If you have a lot of data to analyze, either in terms of cases or variables, you will probably find it necessary to use a mainframe computer to conduct statistical analysis. Of course, the relative advantages of the use of a large computer can be dramatically reduced by an overloaded time-sharing operating system, unreliability of hardware or software, poor turn-around time in acquiring output, or restricted access to terminals or programs. If your data base is large enough, however, you can find that a mainframe computer is really your only choice. Analysis of census data, or the Survey Research Center's *Panel Study of Income Dynamics,* for example, stretch the capacity of even moderately large mainframe computers, and are clearly beyond the capabilities of present micros.

Likewise, some types of research require the speed and accuracy of large machines, or can utilize the resources of big multi-user systems more efficiently than those of microcomputers. Monte Carlo studies, numerical analyses, and complex simulations often need hours of processing time on mainframe or superminicomputers (which might stretch into *days* on a microcomputer), and frequently use extended precision mathematics, large array storage, or other facilities that are currently not widely available for micros. Analyses like these are probably most efficiently conducted in a "batch" mode on a multi-user system, in which they can run undisturbed by other processes, still allowing these other programs a share of the computer's attention. Even this procedure is not sufficient for some problems, however. Although rare in the social and behavioral sciences, analyses requiring the undivided attention of a large mainframe, or even a supercomputer like a Cray-2, are not uncommon in physics and mathematics.

Another problem that frequently plagues microcomputer users is that the kind of software needed to conduct analyses either is not yet available, or is prohibitively expensive for their machines. Statistical software often falls into these categories. For any of these reasons, then, you might find it desirable or even necessary to depend upon a larger computer to conduct your data analysis. This does *not* mean, though, that your microcomputer has become an albatross.

In previous sections of this book, we have discussed communications programs for microcomputers, and their ability to make your micro-computer appear to a mainframe as a terminal. Depending on your communications software (and, to a lesser extent, on the mainframe), you can use your micro as either a "dumb" or "smart" terminal. As a dumb terminal, your micro will emulate one of the terminals employed by others who use the mainframe, and give you comparable access to the mainframe's resources. With smart terminal software, however, your microcomputer becomes a much more powerful tool.

If the data you wish to analyze are stored on disk, for example, you may be able to upload them quickly, and virtually error-free, to a storage device on the mainframe, while your terminal-bound colleagues will have to enter, or pay someone to enter, their data, probably by hand. If you have collected your data through one of the automated processes that we have discussed, you're even further ahead in the game.

If you have to write a program, whether a file of control cards for a statistical package or a "real" program in FORTRAN or some other languge, you can write it using your word processing software or other file editor, and upload it to the mainframe just as you uploaded your data. Your colleagues, meanwhile, might have to struggle to find a terminal that is not in use, and then contend with poor response time using the mainframe's file editor.

When you get the results of your analysis, you can download them to your micro, and store them on your disk. You can edit them at your leisure using your word processor, and merge them into the text of your paper. You can back up your disks quickly and cheaply, and store them in a safe place, while your colleagues have to rerun their analyses to replace lost results.

All these advantages accrue to you just by using your microcomputer as a smart terminal. If you add to this the ability of your micro to conduct at least part of your analysis independently of the mainframe, you can see that a microcomputer is extraordinarily useful even when not used to do "heavy duty" statistical analysis. If we can look forward to having desktop-size machines with the capacity of today's mainframes in the near future, microcomputers begin to look like serious research tools.

For Further Reading

As mentioned before, there are dozens of statistical packages for microcomputers available, and many other useful software products for data analysis. Good sources of reviews of these kinds of products are the *Social Science Micro Review,* published at North Carolina State University and *The ICPSR MicroNews* from the Institute for Social Research, University of Michigan. The Michigan State University Department of Agricultural Economics has published two reports evaluating statistical software for microcomputers that are of great utility. Some other useful reviews are in Carpenter et al. (1984), Grafton and Permaloff (1983), and Katz (1983).

6. WRITING THE RESEARCH REPORT

The production of research reports—conference papers, articles, monographs, books—is the logical culmination of a research project. In some ways, it is anticlimactic: writing up the results of the research may be the least exciting part of the project work. Yet it is also crucial. Your research peers learn most completely about the results of your research project through the written reports you produce. Perceptions of the quality of your research will be disproportionately shaped by the quality of the written reports of that research.

We reiterate that microcomputers cannot make good writers of bad ones, although they probably can make reports of even bad research look good typographically. What they can do is make the production of the report text much easier through the use of a word processor, and further assist you with your report writing by helping you prepare and manage citations and bibliographies, check for spelling and typographical errors, and find and correct certain kinds of grammatical mistakes. In addition, they can facilitate your search for a better word through an electronic thesaurus, and "automatically" prepare tables of contents and indexes.

Microcomputer Word Processing (Again!)

There is little need to go into the use of microcomputer word processors to prepare the research report. Writing a research report is not significantly different from writing a research proposal. All the features of micro word processors that were cited as useful in preparing research proposals are also useful in preparing research reports. Indeed, given that research reports are likely to be longer than proposals or that there will be several reports resulting from a single proposal, a word processor will undoubtedly save even more time in report writing than in proposal preparation.

One or two points may be worth additional emphasis at this point, however. First, most researchers—especially those in the social sciences and humanities—find that even an excellent research report will require resubmission to a publisher at least once before a final version is accepted for publication. Sometimes the resubmission is prepared for the same journal after editorial review indicates that certain changes are desirable. At other times, the resubmission comes after a report has been rejected for publication in a particular outlet.

In the first case—a "revise and resubmit"—the word processor will simply make the execution of the desired changes faster and easier. A handsome revised version of the report can be prepared and resubmitted with relative ease. In the case of a resubmission following a rejection, the word processor can be of even greater benefit. First, if useful suggestions for revisions have been made, they can be incorporated easily into the report just as in the case of a "revise and resubmit." Second, the word processor can save immense amounts of time that might otherwise have to be expended to change the *style* of a rejected report to make it suitable for submission to the publication that may be most appropriate for a second submission, but that may use a completely different style from the first. B.w.p. (before word processing) authors (including us) at least occasionally submitted rejected articles to journals that were not their optimum choices for a second submission simply because they used the same style as the journal for which the report had initially been prepared. Submissions to these journals could be accomplished with a minimum of redrafting and retyping of text, notes, and references. A.w.p. (after word processing) the effort required to change the style of an existing manuscript is far less forbidding.

Citation and Bibliography Management

One of the most burdensome parts of research report writing is the preparation and management of footnotes or other citations and bibliographies or lists of references. Almost any experienced researcher will have had the unpleasant experience of finding an error in the footnotes or citations of a carefully proofread article even as late in the process of publication as galley or page proofreading, when such errors may be quite difficult to correct properly. If you are a careful researcher, such errors occur because the preparation of footnotes or citations can be such an interference in the writing of text that you tend to put off or ignore it with the intention of coming back to it later, after the current paragraph, page, section or chapter has been drafted. When you do get back to it, you may have a difficult time remembering exactly what a particular citation was supposed to be, verifying that there is a footnote number in the text for every set of footnote text and a set of footnote text for every footnote number in the text, and so on.

Microcomputer word processors or "add-on" programs designed to work with them can make footnote and citation preparation easier and more reliable. Some word processing systems have the ability to handle automatically footnote text within their ordinary text formatting routines. An example is the popular Perfect Writer. Others—WordStar, for example—do not have a native ability to automatically handle footnotes, but can be augmented by "add-on" programs such as Footnote, that give them that capability. In either case, footnote text is entered directly into the ordinary text at the time it is freshest in your mind. Special markers set it off so that it will be recognized and printed in the appropriate place—the bottom of the page, the end of the document, wherever—when the report is printed by the text formatter. A consequence of this approach, which many micro users might find undesirable, is that the on-screen display of WordStar (and similar programs) loses much of its display accuracy. Line counts and page breaks are thrown off, for example. The display becomes more like that of the word processors with command-driven text formatters and limited on-screen formatting. Nevertheless, the increase in the ease of citation preparation that results may be worth the price in on-screen display accuracy.

Spelling and Typographical Error Checking

Not all researchers are good spellers, and probably only a very few can type without making a substantial number of typographical errors. Checking report text for spelling and typographical errors is a burdensome task that can be made much easier with the help of a microcomputer "spelling checker." A spelling checker is a program that reads electronic text and checks each word against one or more dictionaries to see if it is present. It assumes that the words it finds in the dictionaries are correctly spelled. It reports the words it does not find for inspection by the human conducting the spelling check. Depending upon the particular spelling checker, the human is then given the option of informing the program that the word is correct and therefore should be ignored, or that it is incorrect and should be corrected. The spelling checker will, at a minimum, mark incorrect words with a special marker so that they can be found and corrected with the text editor. Some will also list possible alternative spellings and correct the incorrect word to correspond with one of the alternative spellings, if so instructed.

Incorrect words may actually be misspelled, or they may simply have been mistyped. In either case, even the most careful writers are often surprised at the ability of spelling checkers to find incorrect spellings even in carefully proofread text. The words the spelling checker lists as possibly misspelled but which are in fact correct, may not be in the checker's dictionary because they are proper names, technical terms, and so on, or simply because no dictionary of reasonable size will contain all the words that you may use in a given report. The spelling checker will ordinarily give you an opportunity to add such words to the principal dictionary or to one or more supplemental dictionaries that the spelling checker can use. It is wise to do this for words that you will use quite often in your writing, but not wise to do it for all the words your spelling checker may incorrectly identify as misspelled. To do so would eventually cause the time required to conduct a normal spelling check to expand so much that you would give up using the checker, because even the fastest spelling checker requires more time to check larger than smaller dictionaries.

We must stress that no spelling checker or "grammar checker" (see below) can obviate the need for careful human proofreading of your documents. Regretfully, current versions of such programs cannot detect wrong words that happen to match dictionary entries (such as the classic "to," "too," and "two," or "effect" and "affect," for example), phrases that make no sense because of omitted or badly arranged words, or many other errors that require an *understanding* of the text to detect.

Grammar Checking

Even though no microcomputer program can substitute for a conscientious human proofreader, another type of program called a "grammar checker" can help a proofreader by identifying certain problems with text or style that can be easily overlooked or that may lie outside the knowledge of the writer or proofreader. Just as even the most talented author may misspell certain words, so may he or she make common stylistic or grammatical mistakes. Grammar checkers can detect important subclasses of such mistakes that will not appear as errors to spelling checkers.

At this stage of the development of microcomputer software, the name "grammar checker" unfortunately promises more than these programs can deliver. They cannot provide a check for the occurrence of even such elementary grammatical mistakes as subject-verb disagreement or improper tense or number. What they can do is help you identify typographical problems like doubled words ("the the"), inconsistent capitalization ("WHat they can do ... "), failure to capitalize the beginning of a sentence, unbalanced quotation marks and parentheses, and so on. In addition, programs like GRAMMATIK can use their own or your specialized phrase dictionaries to identify cliches, poor choices of words, some kinds of poor sentence structure, sexist phrases, and so on. Finally, by compiling for you a list of each different word in a document and a count of the number of times it occurs, they can help you identify possibly overworked words, and by calculating average word and sentence lengths they may help you identify potential readability problems. Currently, style-checking programs that spot undesirable writing characteristics are available on mainframe and minicomputers. We can expect that these kinds of programs will be developed for microcomputers as well, although they will probably require at least 256K memory and possibly a hard disk system. Similarly, programs for the preparation of tables and the typesetting of equations can be expected soon. Several word processors for microcomputers, including Proofwriter, permit the entry and editing of equations using superscripts, subscripts, and a full range of mathematical and scientific symbols.

Electronic Thesaurus

A final writing tool that now exists in an easy-to-use electronic form is the thesaurus. Some text editors have the ability to allow you to access an electronic thesaurus to search for alternatives for any particular word marked by the cursor during text entry or editing. Once accessed, the thesaurus program displays its listing of alternative words for the highlighted words and may even replace the original word with your choice of an alternative before returning you to the text editor.

Automatic Tables of Contents and Indexes

The production of a detailed table of contents or a proper index for a long research report can take a substantial amount of time. It is possible to save much of this time through the use of automated table of contents and index production functions available in some command-driven microcomputer word processors and in add-on programs for "what you see is what you get" word processors like WordStar. Such programs usually require you to enter special markers to identify topical headings to be included in a table of contents or in a document index. The markers may be entered as the text is input or on a subsequent edit of the text. Although they are visible on the screen, the markers ordinarily do not otherwise affect the on-screen display of "what you see is what you get" text formatters; for instance, line and column counts and page breaks remain accurate. Once they are in place, the text formatter or a special purpose program will process the text and print out a properly formatted table of contents or index to accompany the text.

NOTES

1. No microcomputer word processing program will likely have *all* the capabilities discussed in this section, even though at least one program has each of them. The best programs provide most of these capabilities in an easy-to-use-format, however. See Figure 2.1 for the features in some representative word processing programs.

2. SUPERFILE is available for CP/M and MS-DOS computers. Nota Bene was at this writing available only for the IBM-PC and PC XT.

3. The file program is by no means limited to recording the amount of information in the example. In principle, it can record up to 32 full screens of information in the form for a single record. In practice, disk storage limitations and access times will generally limit your ability to create note files nearly as large as the file program's potential limits.

REFERENCES

ABBOTT, J. L. (1983) "A comparison of five database management programs." BYTE 8 (May): 220-231.

AHL, D. H. (1984) "How to buy an electronic spreadsheet." Creative Computing 10 (June): 83-98.

ALLSWANG, J. M. (1983a) "Operating systems: an abundance of options." Interface Age 8(September): 60-66, 167.

———(1983b) "Operating systems: what the user needs to know." Interface Age 8 (August): 54-57, 162.

BARAS, E. M. (1984) The Osborne/McGraw-Hill Guide to Using Lotus 1-2-3. Berkeley, CA: Osborne/Mc-Graw Hill.

CARPENTER, J., D. DELORIA, and D. MORGANSTEIN (1984) "Statistical software for microcomputers" BYTE 9 (April): 234-264.

DATE, C. J. (1983) Database, A Primer. Reading, MA: Addison-Wesley.

DERFLER, F. Jr. and W. STALLINGS (1983) A Manager's Guide to Local Networks. Englewood Cliffs, NJ: Prentice-Hall.

GLOSSBRENNER, A. (1983) The Complete Handbook of Personal Computer Communications. New York: St. Martin's.

GOOD, P. I. (1982) Choosing A Word Processor. Reston, VA: Reston Publishing.

GRAFTON, C. and A. PERMALOFF (1983) "Statistical packages for personal computers." PS 16 (Spring): 182-188.

HEINTZ, C. (1984) "Solving the data base puzzle." Interface Age 9 (February): 58-69.

———(1983a) "Guide to database system software." Interface Age 8 (February): 52-67. 148-150.

———(1983b) "Operating systems: deciding what's best for you." Interface Age 8 (October): 76-82, 165-168.

———(1983c) "Seeking solutions with spreadsheets." Interface Age 8 (September): 52-59.

———(1982a) "Buyer's guide to word processing software." Interface Age 7 (December): 40-58.

———(1982b) "Evaluation of financial planning packages." Interface Age 7 (July): 78-93.

HEISER, P. W. (1984) Mastering dBase II the Easy Way. Englewood Cliffs, NJ: Prentice-Hall.

HOPKINS, K. D. and G. V GLASS (1978) Basic Statistics for the Behavioral Sciences. Englewood Cliffs, NJ: Prentice-Hall.

KATZ, J. A. (1983) "Statistical programs for Apple computers." The ICPSR MicroNews 1 (September).

JORDAN, L. E. and B. CHURCHILL (1983) Communications and Networking for the IBM PC. Bowie, MD: Robert J. Brady.

LOCKWOOD, R. (1984) "Choosing and using a word processor." Creative Computing 10 (December): 126-145.

MADRON, T. W. (1984) Local Area Networks in Large Organizations. Hasbrouch Heights, NJ: Hayden.
———(1983) Microcomputers in Large Organizations. Englewood Cliffs, NJ: Prentice-Hall.
———(1969) Small Group Methods and the Study of Politics. Evanston, IL: Northwestern University Press.
———and C. N. TATE (1984) Your T.I. Professional Computer: Use, Applications and BASIC. New York: Holt Rinehart & Winston.
MALLOY, R., G. M. VOSE, and T. CLUNE (1984) "The IBM PC AT." BYTE 9 (October): 108-111.
McWILLIAMS, P. (1982) The Word Processing Book. Los Angeles: Prelude Press.
MOSTELLER, F. and M. WALLACE (1964) Inference and Disputed Authorship: The Federalist. Reading, MA: Addison-Wesley.
NICHOLS, E. A., J. C. NICHOLS, and K. R. MUSSON (1982) Data Communications for Microcomputers. New York: McGraw-Hill.
NILLES, J. M. (1983) Micros and Modems: Telecommunicating with Personal Computers. Reston, VA: Reston Publishing.
PALMER, W.J. (1983) "Microcomputers in survey research." Interface Age 8 (December): 69-74.
SCHRODT, P. A. (1984) Microcomputer Methods for Social Scientists. University Paper series, Quantitative Applications in the Social Sciences, 07-001. Beverly Hills, CA: Sage.
SHUFORD, R.S. (1983) "Word tools for the IBM personal computer." BYTE 8 (November): 176-202.
STONE, P. J. (1966) The General Inquirer: A Computer Approach to Content Analysis. Cambridge: MIT Press.
STULTZ, R. A. (1984) The Illustrated Multiplan Book. Englewood Cliffs, NJ: Prentice-Hall.
WELLS, P. (1984) "The 80286 microprocessor." BYTE 9 (November): 221-242.

THOMAS WM. MADRON is Manager of Computer Services and Professor of Political Science at North Texas State University. He received his undergraduate education at Westminster College, his M.A. from American University, and his Ph.D. from Tulane University. He also holds a Certificate in Data Processing. He has published articles on the history of religion, political behavior, and political parties in such journals as American Sociological Review, Public Opinion Quarterly, *and* Methodist History, *and articles on computing in such journals as* BYTE *and* Kilobaud Microcomputing. *His books include* Small Group Methods and the Study of Politics *(1969),* Political Parties in the United States *(1974, with Chelf) and* Local Area Networks in Large Organizations *(1984), among others. He is a regular columnist for* Computerworld.

C. NEAL TATE is Professor and Chairperson of Political Science at North Texas State University. He received his undergraduate education at Wake Forest University and his graduate degrees from Tulane University. He has published articles on research methodology, political behavior, and judicial politics in such journals as American Political Science Review *and* Political Behavior. *He is co-author, with T. W. Madron, of* Your TI Professional Computer: Use, Applications and BASIC, *and the forthcoming* Improving Productivity with Tandy MS-DOS Computers. *He is currently involved in research in the comparative study of judiciaries.*

ROBERT G. BROOKSHIRE is Manager of Academic Computing and Assistant Professor of Political Science at North Texas State University. He received his undergraduate education at the University of Georgia, his master's degree from Georgia State University, and his Ph.D. from Emory University. He has published articles on research methodology and the U.S. Congress in such journals as Legislative Studies Quarterly. *He is currently involved in research on career patterns in the House and Senate.*

Quantitative Applications
in the Social Sciences

(a Sage University Papers Series)

$6.00 each

SAGE PUBLICATIONS, INC.
P.O. BOX 5024
BEVERLY HILLS, CALIFORNIA 90210

Place
Stamp
here